# COSMIC PROPHECIES

# FOR THE YEAR 2,000

**A Channeled Symposium On What We Can Expect For The Rest Of The Decade**

**Compiled through TUELLA through the Ashtar Command**

ISBN: 0-938294-23-7

Editorial Direction
& Layout:
Timothy Green Beckley

Composition and design:
Cross-Country Consultants
8858 E. Palm Ridge Drive
Scottsdale, AZ 85260

For permission to reprint specific portions or to inquire
about foreign rights, address request to Inner Light,
Box 753, New Brunswick, NJ 08903

Free catalog of books upon request.

# Contents

# Foreword

The plan for this book has existed on spiritual levels for considerable time. That moment has come when we of the Hierarchy now focus our energies for its manifestation, upon the physical plane.

The words go forth on the Authority of the Great White Brotherhood and under my sponsorship. We release them in a simplicity that all might understand. Included in the Cosmic Symposium are those who represent the Angel Kingdom, the Great Central Sun Government, the Heavenly Host, the Great Karmic Board, the Chohans of Earth Solar System, Universal Masters, and the great Alliance of the Intergalactic Confederation.

In my "three times three, times three" assembly of twenty-seven speakers, there is a great variety of approach to our theme, from many rays of expression. Yet a divine thread intertwines through all, in a united warning of the times and a spiritual call to preparedness. These fall easily into the four divisions as presented, which I have coined my "volume foursquare."

They are not designed for eloquence, entertainment or intellectual fare. Neither profound nor prophetic, but rather timely and emphatic. They are lowered into the physical octave specifically for preparing certain souls who are now ready to receive them. The sentences should be read very slowly, and the messages thrice read, for the maximum of Light they carry, to be absorbed by the inner being.

Many invited to speak were unable to participate on the days appointed. Others have graciously rearranged their personal schedules to respond.

Our messenger has prepared herself for this assignment for many lifetimes, in a cooperative effort with Cosmic Intelligences. I express my gratitude to her and my appreciation to each Great Soul who has contributed their thoughts to our messenger that the work might be compiled and released on schedule. I send my Blessings and my Love to all who look upon these words of Light.

Your sponsor,
Kuthumi

# Preface

The content of this volume stands on its own merits. I do not justify it or in any way come to its defense. It will defend itself.

I do not debate, nor argue with anyone, or apologize for any message which is delivered through me. I am only a messenger. To those who do not seek, no argument is possible. To those who do, no argument is necessary.

These messages were received through mental telepathic impression, while fully conscious, assisted by Tensor Beam from higher dimensions and from interdimensional and interplanetary spacecraft.

The vocal communications have been tape recorded as they were delivered and later transcribed as presented herein.

Read not to contradict, nor to believe and take for granted, but to weigh and consider.

**The messenger,**
**Tuella**

# Section One
# World Chaos

## The Cloud of Chaos

Its detonations ravish all
Within its sphere
Of awful devil light,
That poisonous mushroom
Created out of fear.

Not satisfied, it creeps
And twists and smashes
Throughout the land,
Across the sky.

Relentlessly and viciously
It lashes out at every form
Of life.
Scientists of note declare—

God give us strength,
The awful burden of our miscreations
Of your forces, Lord, to bear,
And guide us back...to where
Your great and wondrous power.

Is only used for good and peace
For love that always gives,
Will not devour.
This mighty, holy, sacred fire—
Created to serve life, rather than
Misdirected desire.

—Eileen Schoen

# An Ultimatum from the Great Central Son

## by The Elohim

"Call unto me and I will answer thee and show thee great and mighty things." I Am That I Am speaketh with thee. I Am the source of all truth, I Am the giver of Life. I Am the cause of all things. I Am within thee and a part of thee and I speak from within thy being, I speak the words as they come from the celestial realms. These are the words from the Most High given thee:

1. We, the Elohim of God, send forth our message on the Planet Earth in this appeal to the flesh of this generation to accept the blessings offered to man by the Elohim of Heaven. Unless humanity is willing to accept the outstretched hand of Love, there will come to this planet spasms of tremendous upheaval and loss of life. The forces of destruction that are within the earth cannot be contained unless your world community will yield itself to a spiritual awakening. Be still and listen to the beat of your hearts, and know that within collective creation, all hearts beat in tempo with your own. Know that all of life finds its source in the pulse of the Universe. The cohesive element of externalization is Love.

2. You have buried within your Being the knowledge of who you are and why you are here and from whence you have come. You have hidden under veils of remoteness and illusion, the glory, the shining splendor of your inner fire and your inner

10

Divinity. Ye are Gods. Ye are created in the power Divine. We, the Elohim of the Highest Throne, invoke the Light that is within each and every one of you, we call it FORTH into MANIFESTATION! We invoke the RELEASE OF LIGHT from every atom of Being.

3. If souls refuse to yield to this Light, the millennium will be delayed, The Age of Peace and Love, and the evolution of the human race could be set back another entire cycle of time, in the history of humanity. The maximum of human suffering will be experienced unless human consciousness will gear itself to reach higher than the present level of spiritual understanding. If they will but call upon God as they understand Him to be, and seek guidance and direction for this decade, their call will be heard and answered. It takes but a call turned heavenward, with the mind and the heart's desire, to find an instant response within the corporate Divinity, known to man as the Elohim.

4. Citizens of Earth have within your governing bodies the framework for setting into motion the dispensation of Love. You have within your International Congress, your United Nations, the machinations of its inner Assemblies, to exercise the decisions of tolerance and peace. Nations are manipulated into battle array through human responses of the human self, overruling the promptings of Divine benevolence and gallantry. Does world society *really* have a choice in these matters? Can you not comprehend that either you will choose the Pathway of Light and Love within your International Assemblies, or you shall walk the Pathway of Darkness and destruction within all nations throughout the planet?

We are combining our persuasiveness to focus this message into terrestrial vibrations, that it will be a stimulus of power, that it will motivate a response from within the souls of mankind. O Man, why will you choose to continue in the pathway of materialism and sensuality as has ever been the trend in crises past? When a challenge has been placed in the pathway

11

of man's evolution toward the Father, it has been the trend of society to choose the comforts, the glamour, the darkness, and the path that leads to deeper regression of the soul.

In our prerogative as the Elohim before the Throne, we call to souls to arise and seek the Pathway of Illumination and Spirituality; right thinking and right values; to choose for the eternal verities and the very salvation of a planet and the souls upon it.

5. The Host of the Celestial Plane will not stand by idly and look upon the wilful destruction of a planet. The Angels of Judgment will move upon the evil genius who would architect the destruction of millions for personal gain. This despotism shall not stand! It shall be removed to the uttermost parts of infinity for an entire cycle of time. We shall send forth this warning to the warmongers upon Earth. Whatever infernal steps toward the mobilization for nuclear hostilities are taken, expect intervention from the Highest Forces of the Universe. We, as a united voice, send forth the fiat: IT SHALL NOT PASS! IT SHALL NOT PASS! IT SHALL NOT PASS! They that would seek to destroy shall themselves be destroyed by their own manipulations.

6. The Order has reverberated throughout the universe that the destruction of Shan shall not be permitted. So, brace yourselves, sons and daughters of the Most High. Brace yourselves, for the opposition of the Dark Ones and the Fallen Ones, for every step they take toward destruction shall be met with Divine Opposition, and great struggles shall ensue between the two forces. Hold yourselves ever within our Brilliancy. Invoke the resplendence of God around your being, your families, your households, and your daily activities. Do not let your force field of Light fall away at ANY TIME. Reinforce it daily, for as the Light increases so shall the Darkness exalt itself. No harm can come to you. No ill can befall you as long as you are filled with Love within, and clothed with your circle of Light without. Fear is for those who abide in the dark-

ness. Faith and assurance are the inheritance of those who walk with the Shining One. FEAR NOT, FOR THIS SHALL PASS QUICKLY.

From the Great Central Sun, beyond your Sun, we send forth to the sons and daughters of God, our Great Halos of blessings, our force field of magnetic protection, and an expansion of all of the Light that surrounds the Planet. We precipitate upon these printed words, wherever they shall be placed, into whosoever's hands, in whatever home, an invisible Golden Thread that reaches upward to our hearts. From here, the Divine Presence of heavenly illumination descends along this thread with velocity into the heart of one who reads, and the home where that one abides. For these are words of Living Light sent forth by the Elohim of God, as messengers to mankind."

**The Elohim Hath Spoken**

## Points to Ponder
### –or–
### (Group Discussion)

I. Earth changes are conditional.
2. Ye are Gods.
3. Be careful of the choices you make.
4. In spite of man, the planet will be saved.
5. Invoke the Light during Armageddon.
6. Divine Presence accompanies Words of Light.

## NOTES:

# The Threshold of Sorrows

## by Mother Mary

Good afternoon, Tuella. I am Mother Mary speaking with you once again, and remembering our wonderful experiences together at Easter time.

1 & 2. I am very pleased to share my brief message today, for the book that is created to be a helping hand, a staff to lean upon, a direction finder, in the decade of the Eighties. You must realize it is with much solemnity and heavy heart that I look upon the plight of my beloved children, as they now stand upon the threshold of the tribulation period, in the cycle of human evolution. I am tossed within my heart for the parents of children, and the youth of the land, and the little ones who follow.

3. Any mother's heart would feel as mine, if she could discern beyond the veil of human carnality and banality, the monstrous plans in the making, that would tear asunder the hope of humanity's ascension. Tremendous themes of wickedness from malevolent forces belch forth their abominations upon the youngsters of this generation. We of the Angelic Kingdom have looked upon the impurities within your halls of learning, and shuddered within ourselves to see the occupation of your children.

4 & 5. The very earth itself, and the stones thereof, will cry out and reel to and fro in planetary sorrow for my little ones. For nature may only bear its portion; the elementals have

15

horizons beyond which they cannot serve the will of man. In that there comes a point in time when the entire nature and mineral kingdoms will revolt against the weight of darkness. Then, my beloved ones, get ye to the hills and the high plains, and take ye what little may be your needs, and hide thyself from the wrath of nature unleashed in your generation.

6. Modern warriors have called forth massive machineries of death to cover the land with their aggressive invasions of life. Let them come. Let them bluster across the land. Let them polish their steel, patrol the seas, and hurl defiance from the skies; it shall come to no avail. For the weapons that are formed against another shall be turned upon those that have formed them. The mentation to destroy, projected toward another, shall be turned again unto the destruction of those who hath sent it. For the earth is the Lord's and the fullness thereof, and the terrestrial entity shall turn against the inhabitants thereof who plot its devastation. As an animal shakes itself free of the waters upon it, so shall creation shake itself free of those who would annihilate it.

7. Many generations have read of these days. Many have come and gone who have studied the words of my beloved Son, but the Words remain to call this day, "Come, ye blessed of My Father, inherit the Kingdom prepared for you from the foundation of the world." The Light of His Love shall go forth like the sunrise, dispelling the darkness of the world's karma; dissolving the mists of confusion, liberating nature to return to its former glory. You, my children, shall be overshadowed by the Angel of His Presence.

8 & 9. Teach thy young the promises of His Protection. Be an example of calmness in chaos, and serenity in the storm. Let them join with you in expecting His blessing and hearing His voice.

For, as they experience Love Divine, Love shall be drawn to them. In all that shall beset you throughout the years of the Eighties, Love shall overshadow my children, and Love shall be

16

your buckler and shield, and, if need be, Love shall be thy token of deliverance. I am the Mother of Beloved Jesus,

Mary

## Points to Ponder
### –or–
### (Group Discussion)

I.   This book is a roadmap.
2.  We are on the threshold of the tribulation.
3.  Our children are in danger!
4.  Revolt of the nature kingdom.
5.  High altitudes recommended.
6.  War plots boomerang.
7.  The calm in the eye of the storm.
8.  Should the children's minds be prepared for possible future changes?
9.  Do I exemplify calmness and serenity in all situations?

**NOTES:**

# Stand Tall in the Trial By Fire

## by El Morya

Good evening, child of light. Greetings in the sign of the Heart, Head and Hand unto you. This is Morya speaking. I do not wish to be omitted from this effort sponsored by my dear brother and friend, Kuthumi, and I am here to keep my appointment as promised. We are all very grateful for your energies that are given to us, for we are greatly in need of the assistance of our chelas in embodiment. As our eyes go to and fro upon the earth, there is ever a search for steadfast souls who will jump into the fray and carry on the battle for Light.

**1.** Now let us consider some things relevant to the decade before your world. The present severe economic upheaval can only go into deeper complications before it can be resolved. We do not anticipate any phenomenal solutions along these lines in the early part of this decade. The thinking of man must aright itself. As right thinking is applied to all the levels of life, humanity will find a change taking place even in the great financial hierarchies of the planet, for man must release all things and exercise his stewardship of wealth along with other responsibilities. The money manipulators and the cartel of energy czars shall be leveled to normal size when the earth is tossed by the winds of change. The centers of Mammon that line many coastlines shall be washed of their contaminations forever.

Presently, and in the immediate future, Cosmic rays are being shed upon your globe that will help to break down the competitive thought forms of humanity, and materialistic avenues of expression. Thought patterns, that ever flow around the planet, will be injected with transfusions of high-level energies, penetrating and affecting the decisions and choices everywhere. These changes wrought on the mental level will generate a friction with existing surrounding thought patterns. Thus, the very atmosphere will vibrate in conflict as thought form clashes against thought form. These clouds of resistance shall be dealt with by a cleansing of the very air itself. Great winds and waters, as forces of cleansing, join their energies to purify the ethers and the astral belt.

2. Then shall come a clearer vision, enabling the citizens of Terra to approach earth's problems from a higher plateau of solution. That day will come when the desert lands shall blossom as the rose, and drought shall be no more. In the New Birth of the land many will grow into greatness and the stature of stalwart sons and daughters of God. At the community level, before that time, brotherhood and concern for neighbor shall be mellowed with love and compassion, as group action increases in response to repeated emergencies.

3. Let us move on. We, the Masters of the Karmic Board, have directed that global war shall not be permitted to destroy this planet. Neither shall the chelas and the watching souls be taken unawares. The fiat of the highest council in the solar system has decreed that no nation shall venture forth upon other nations in a manner that would lead to the annihilation of the earth itself. Watchmen ever guarding, ever patrolling the actions and decisions of the secret councils of the nations, are never without complete and full awareness of all proposals and plans. Any action that leads into disturbances on an interplanetary level, shall precipitate Divine Intervention and retaliating disciplines. The Universal decree, now in effect, provides for Unity and Peace throughout the Solar System and the Alliance

of the Universes. This Cosmic Law shall be enforced by the Angelic Forces under the administration of the Blue Ray of Will and Power.

Know ye not that those events of cataclysmic nature, which the time tables of men have scheduled to appear at the close of this century, have now been stepped up, and they shall become the instruments of Divine Intervention, if the course of humanity is bent on nuclear destruction. Blazing paths of fire, flaming across the darkened sky, in thunderings of awesome sights never before experienced by man in his evolutions, shall be the harvest resulting from the perversion of planetary energies.

4. You have studied your heavens. You have seen the setting of the stage overhead, in the stationing of the rendezvous of the starry bodies. To the wise the guidance is written. Yet man, with the flame of life burning within, and a spiritual desire to turn from genocide and debauchery, can overrule by 'the momentum of reversal, and the authority of embodiment can overrule, I say, the very stars in their courses, by the Power of His call to us.

5. I am El Morya. I administrate unto you the manifestation of Divine Will and Power. Call upon me, and I will release, within the entire being, a strengthening of Will and Determination, that will cause my chelas to stand tall in the trial by fire, and come from it without even the smell of smoke upon them. Fear not what man shall do to thee, if thy determinations are fixed upon thy starry destiny. Hold thy staff of faith firmly, and face the winds of tribulation as they come. Take your stand for Right-ness, and having done all, STAND; in the Power of the Will of El Morya who bathes thy four lower bodies in the Blue Flame of Protection, for Deliverance in this decade. Choose ye, to be willing to be made willing, to walk the pathway of the Ascended Masters which shines in splendor as a ribbon of Light, cutting through the densities of darkness that settle upon the world.

I am saluting all who read my words,

El Morya

## Points to Ponder
### -or-
## (Group Discussion)

I. Can negative thought levels affect world economies?
2. Community togetherness in disaster.
3. Nuclear war will precipitate Divine Intervention in the form of cataclysms.
4. Is it within the power of mankind to weaken these forces?
5. How are the chelas of the Masters protected?

## NOTES:

# The Invisible Fortress
# of Love

## by Archangel Michael

Hail to you, O daughter of God! I am Michael, the Archangel of Protection. I am He who carries the mighty sword of Blue Flame, for the protection of America and the souls of Light everywhere upon the planet.

1 & 2. I am integrating the forces of Light, with a blending ray of Blue Flame throughout the planet to encourage these forces to begin to think as one and work in unison, to join forces against the tides of evil. Armageddon and the battle for men's minds is upon us. We of the Celestial realms have moved into close proximity to the planet for the purpose of perpetuating the Blue flame wherever it is needed.

3 & 4. When the dark clouds of thought forms of war, or international emergencies gather in the heavens surrounding the Earth, it is our concerted action and the action of the Blue Flame which disperses and scatters these clouds, weakening or dissolving their propulsions and destructive energies. The momentum toward nuclear global conflict polarizing upon the planet, is not an idle threat. There remains continuing danger to the world from those who do not project their thinking beyond their own horizon. The time has come when men of military stature, and the statesmen of the world, must look beyond the security of their own borders, and carefully weigh

the threat to humanity everywhere of their decisions. There are forces at work upon the planet, which left to their own devices and the fulfillment of the greed of their hearts, would of a certainty, lead to the eradication of an entire planet. THIS HAS HAPPENED BEFORE IN THE HISTORY OF THE SOLAR SYSTEM, BUT IT SHALL NOT HAPPEN AGAIN!

5. The Angelic Host has received orders from on high, that the earth shall be spared as if by a miracle, from the expulsions of dark minds. As these emanations of darkness would rise up against the great rising tide of Light, there shall be a reverberating reaction within the planet itself and its surrounding atmospheres, so that great uncontrollable fusions and eruptions shall give echo to the spiritual imbalance in your environments.

6. Nevertheless, the Angels of God shall stand beside the children of Light wherever circumstances have placed them, as guardians and protectors of the invincible sons and daughters of God. Let fear not be found among you. Fear hath no place in the heart filled with Light and Love. As your planet enters its next dimension, many will fall or be taken, or meet with mishap, right up to your very doors. Stand ye in faith and Love, calling upon the Angels of God to stand with you and invoke the circle of Blue Flame around your home, your entire situation, until this too shall pass.

7. Realize, as you hear the rumblings of threatened war and the rumors of war or prophecies of dire things to come, and the call to preparedness against those days, know ye within your hearts, that it shall not come nigh thee who walk in love with thy brethren and thy neighbor. For Love is a fulfillment of the Christ Presence within every man. Love is the seal of protection. Love is the impenetrable armor. Love is the invincible fortress that cannot be penetrated by the destroyer. Take heart that though for a little while there shall be turmoil and chaos, it is for a little season and for Divine purpose. If thine own heart is purified by the Presence of Love, then Peace shall reign within thine own world, despite the confusion that

24

surrounds you.

I speak upon my Authority as Governor of this Solar System presiding over the solar consciousness of Will and Power. I have sent forth the command that those having that Seal of Light and Love, shall have the assistance and protection of every member of the Angelic Host, for I remain, your Protector,

**Archangel Michael**

## Points to Ponder
### –or–
## (Group Discussion)

I. Forces of Light are to be integrated. Unity essential.
2. Angels closer to earth from now on.
3. War momentum dispersed by Blue Flame.
4. The planet is to be spared.
5. Nature echoes the spiritual imbalance of humanity.
6. Our "Protectors" must be called.
7. Love is the answer.
8. The Seal in the forehead (Rev. 7:2).

## NOTES:

# The Balanced Ledger

## by Saint Germain

I greet you in the flame of my being. I am known as St. Germain on planetary levels, and Elihu in celestial realm. I place my blessing upon this volume foursquare, sent forth by the Brotherhood, under the sponsoring of my friend Kuthumi, World Teacher. It is my privilege to have been given this opportunity to speak.

**1.** We of the Great Karmic Board have much to deliberate concerning the coming decade for the world. All things progress under Divine Will. Some things are permitted, others are ordained to be. There is an unbalanced ledger in the name of this nation which cannot be tampered with. Nevertheless, we do extend mercy and compassion in all of our decisions and extend all possible leniency in administrating our final decrees.

**2.** The listening angels and the angel with the writer's inkhorn by his side, fail not to tally every intention and provocation of the human heart. Souls cluster in groups, around an ideology or a principle, and become nations. As nations, their group karma for good or ill, is registered in the great heavenly records. America has accumulated great good through many centuries of benevolence toward all, with a friendliness, and an inclination toward the ongoing Light of God and the principles of freedom.

**3.** In a broad aspect these principles have been maintained and upheld. But in the last two decades, there has been an alarming trend away from those principles instituted by the founders of America. Questionable alliances have been encouraged. The foundation of the currency has been allowed to flow into dangerous shoals of threatening shipwreck of the economy. Hidden malignant forces have been permitted to seize inner control of the government.

4. The principles under God that made this nation an instrument of Light, have suffered at the hands of infiltrators who have betrayed the spirit of the true American heritage. The watchmen have slept at their post and the guardsmen have winked their eye, but the hand of the angel with the writer's inkhorn by his side, writes on.

With all of our great extended mercy, there is a record, yet to be reckoned with by America, which only the Great Lawgiver can balance. The destiny of this nation under God, as a shining star in the firmament, shall not be denied. A cleansing tide shall sweep the land of the debris of the dark ones. From the highest office in the land to the lowly cabin upon the mountainside, purity and dedication to one nation under God shall motivate the deeds of all that dwell therein. That which is better shall supplant that which is lesser, and new golden cities shall dot the terrain.

5. The face of the land shall change, but the hearts of the citizens shall be united in the manifestation of brotherly love and goodwill. The birth pangs of a New Age will bring a moment of travail, it is true, but that travail shall soon be forgotten in the joy of a New World in all of its beauty. As you face the coming decade, know that the balancing shall be accomplished. Those who have given their energies, and their time and talents toward the higher way of life and to the incoming Light, shall have the security and protection under the canopy of the Ascended Masters of America. The great beings and super-intelligences that have guided an America down through the centuries shall, in this time of restoration, project a pillar of cloud of their Presence to all those who have

known their names.

I have endowed the planet with the glowing, transmuting violet flame, and my violet angels know the identity and the whereabouts of every soul who has ever called my name. My electronic presence is beside those who read my words. Call upon the transmuting violet flame in cleansing action to perpetuate the purification of your environment and your world. I remain, your benefactor,

St. Germain

## Points to Ponder
### –or–
## (Group Discussion)

I.  America's descending karma tempered with mercy but cannot be cancelled.
2.  Group souls and karma.
3.  Give examples of the decline of national spiritual principles.
4.  What was the American Heritage?
5.  What are the birth pangs of New Age?
6.  The Divine Presence.

## NOTES:

# The Orbit of Destiny

## by Lord Maitreya

**1.** I am Maitreya. I am your speaker for this hour. My words come to you out of the Great Central Sun and the sovereignty of the Great Cosmic Government. I am the Voice of that Government. I bring the blessing of the Most High and the Heavenly Host, with my coming and my words.

**2.** On this beautiful afternoon I will speak concerning the orbit of destiny that has been ordained for the planet earth since time began. For all worlds find their divine pathway, their foreordained destiny by order of the Creator. The world in which you abide must follow its foreordained direction into a new orbit of time and space. With the ending of the old and the beginning of the new, the entrance upon these pathways of destiny is written in the books of heaven and they must come to pass.

**3.** The orb of Terra has leaned itself awry for much too long. The day of reckoning and setting into place is upon you. No living being can alter the course that is decreed for the future of the world. The time of travail cannot be bypassed, for the birth of the New Order must come. That which has been, has not reflected the Divine Plan. But the Plan shall be fulfilled when all things are made right. The heavens sing together for joy in anticipation of that exalted Day, when the mighty lines of force shall be aligned once again. Vast vortices of energy shall spiral from the chakras of the globe and the Kingdom of God with all the lesser kingdoms shall dwell in harmony and peace, and no more shall the earth groan within itself.

4. Tremendous magnetic forces released from within, shall attract to the earth all of the necessary energies required to transform it to a place of beauty and love, once again. It must be, that polarity be wedded with purpose and that all of the planet and those thereon shall live for the Glory of the Most High.

I, Maitreya, invest the planet with my own momentum and surround it with my force field of Perfection. It shall be glorified in all of its beauty as it was intended to be by the Creator. It shall be cleansed of all that is unlike the glowing Light and that which is not a part of that Light shall be separated from its midst. Those who have proven themselves worthy of that Light shall inherit the New Earth to inaugurate the New Dispensation. Rejoice in the Day of the Lord and the Day of the Perfecting of all things. Externalities may end, but your planet shall merge on the pathway to its destiny as a place prepared for beings of Light and Love. A place worthy of those who shall inhabit it.

5. I, Maitreya, pour my vial of cleansing flame upon the planet, that Divine Will shall be fulfilled. Under Universal Law all negative manifestation precipitated upon the earth by the will of man, must defer to divine cleansing action. The divine right of personal choice, endowed upon all creation, will inexorably set into motion the cleansing of itself.

It is ordained that those who choose not to enter the new environment, shall not be forced to do so, but quite to the contrary, shall be escorted to a place prepared according to their choices.

The fiat of Light has been released, and that Day must come. I am,

**Maitreya**

## Points to Ponder
### –or–
### (Group Discussion)

I. The Greater System billions of miles away, around which seven solar systems revolve together.
2. There are 12 fields of expression, and a difference of Cosmic energies received with different vibratory rats. Our own solar system is presently leaving the Piscean field and entering the Aquarian field of expression and new vibrations.
3. Chakras of the planet become source of great energy supply where New Age cities will be located.
4. A new earth.
5. Planetary karma.

## NOTES:

# The Masters of Invocation

## by Hilarion

1. Good evening. I am Hilarion. I have come to share some of my thoughts for the little book and to add my blessings to those already extended to its readers. I speak concerning the need at this hour for fifth ray energies to be manifested upon and through mankind.

I am calling for a great outpouring of spiritual renewal upon the earth. Many hundreds of Great Beings are gathered in my Emerald City, working together in the projection of thought upon the planet in the manifestation of the green ray of life. These Great Ones, who serve with me, gather together in the Great Hall of my Temple, and meditate upon the need of those who have chosen the Pathway of Light. There are many souls who stand at the very doors of an awakening of their spiritual awareness and spiritual gifts, which they have earned over many lifetimes by their earnestness and sincere seeking, and the application of right principles to life.

2. In the Higher Octave, we meditate and visualize the expansion of that Light, the expansion of awareness of your spiritual birthright and your God Presence within. We concentrate and meditate upon the human potential as embodied sons and daughters of God. We invoke the Light that your dominion and your Mastery shall flow through your entire being. Then indeed shall the earth be filled with Glory!

3. I do not choose to dwell upon unpleasant aspects of the

coming days which contribute to the cleansing of the planet, but rather, I elect to discuss the great benefits that are imminent. Eyes have not seen, ears have not heard, nor can the imagination conceive of the great blessings that await the inspired one through the incoming vibrations and spiritual rays that are to be applied on inner levels. The Most Beloved Master has given a promise along these lines with these words: "Blessed are they which do hunger and thirst after righteousness, for they shall be filled—blessed are the meek, for they shall inherit the earth."

4. I would speak of the ongoing of the Light upon the planet and the faithfulness of the dedicated Light Workers. Until such time as the night cometh when no man can work, you are our hands and feet and our very presence in the physical octave. Without each and every one of you and those that come, our Plans would be without an anchor, and our hopes for mankind would be curtailed. But because we have hearts such as yours, who have chosen to read this very book, we of the etheric realms can know that the salt of the earth continues its work. We can WIN—as long as the children of Light fulfill their mission and stand undaunted by opposition, discouragement, and threats of changes to come. We know that as long as we have this anchor represented by all of you, the Light cannot fail!

There are many discordant voices in the land today who know nothing of the inner meaning of the Light upon the planet. Many who go their way in self pursuits and ill-conceived projections for their future, do not reckon with the invocations of Light that go forth from my Temple Hall. These Great Ones are gathered daily, hourly, to invoke the coming of Light upon the planet Earth. They invoke the presence of Light in the great meetings of your governing bodies and invoke the infiltration of light throughout all the lower kingdoms—the kingdom of the air and of the sea, and all of nature. The incoming Light of God shall accommodate itself to the diverse needs during the planetary cleansing. The Light shall work with this cleansing in a positive way, where positiveness is present.

The Masters of Invocation of the Fifth Ray have declared and sent forth the fiat that the Light of Earth shall expand, expand, expand. In the given momentum of the times, souls will discover great spiritual strength to fearlessly face the challenge of the coming decade. Look neither to the right nor to the left, but steadfastly fix thy gaze upon thy deliverance.

5. It is written that in those days no man shall teach his neighbor, for all shall be guided by the Spirit within. My friends, that day is upon you. When the preparation has finished and the turmoil has ceased, all shall hear the whispering Voice saying, "This is the way; walk therein." Then a great sigh shall come forth from all of creation, when the natural openings of Spirit shall be cleared, manifesting the blessings of the Fifth Ray upon humanity. The gifts which have been sought for so long shall be found and realized by the fulfillment of these things.

Blessed are they who findeth the way and who can consciously face the decade to come in absolute confidence and peace within. Know that beyond the Cross of these times will come the glory of a new earth, a new world, to shine as a new star in the fermament. We are holding YOU in that Great Light. I Am,

Hilarion

## Points to Ponder
### –or–
### (Group Discussion)

I. Fifth Ray energies vital during transition period.
2. The power of creative meditation.
3. "Greater works..." and limitless blessings.
4. God's Infantry.
5. Man is his own teacher.

## NOTES:

# Section Two
# World Changes

## The Focus of Change

A new birthing is imminent
Which transcends all understanding
Of life as we know it on earth.
The planets are lining up,
Waiting for orders
To march in procession.

A grand scheme of the Universe
Is making its claim,
As each one falls in place
In ordered succession.
What powers there be
That call spheres by their name!

To move out in action—
To further the Plan
Of God's Divine Purpose
Created for man.
So let us stand steadfast
And welcome the changes

That will help us to grow
Into more understanding
Of all of His ways;
Let's welcome His fiery
Celestial show!

—Eileen Schoen

# The Fall of
# Exterior Religion

## by ESU (Jesus The Christ)

**1 & 2.** My name is ESU on Celestial levels, known to earth as Jesus the Christ. I Am the Way, the Truth and the Life. For these many centuries, I have looked upon the souls of men as they scurry hither and yon upon the earth, striving with their ambitions, forcing themselves forward in their desire for self esteem. I have watched with much disheartenment as the institutions which bear My Name have long forsaken My Principles and overlooked My Teachings. I have stood by in the shadows, while those intended to represent My Work and My Words have forsaken Me utterly in their struggles for political place among their fellows. I have seen hunger within the hearts of those who have come into these edifices and I have watched them go their way unfilled.

**3.** While great human need on a mass level prevails throughout the planet, I have observed the spending of vast sums of millions and millions of dollars on temples of stone that men might glory thereby, but these shall crumble in the dust. This ostentatiousness in My Name has grieved my heart again and again. I did not give My Life for such as this. I did not come to be made into a God. I came as one of you, to show you the Divine Possibilities that abide within every human life. I came to show the Way, the Path, the Truth, but the world has chosen to exalt Me and My Name, but to ignore and forsake My Teachings of the inner kingdom.

4. There has come One to take up My Work within the hearts of humanity. The Christ Presence within each soul, continues to lead and to show the Way. This is My Contact and My Outreach to every soul upon the planet. As you pay homage to the Christ Presence within your neighbor and your brother, you pay homage to Me and My Words. As you extend the Love of God around your planet to all in need of that Love, you extend your Love to Me. There is so much talk of Christianity upon the earth, but so little of the Presence of the spirit of Christ. Churchianity abounds and divisions compound within it. But there is so little of My Teaching in action in the life of humanity.

5. But all of this will change as the earth is born into a New Day. *Exterior religion will fall away* and inner awareness will become the strength of those who follow Me. I shall walk with them and be in their midst, for they shall endure.

6. I speak of the ramifications of all that is involved in the immediate years before you, of all that is to be in these latter days. Many shall be moved by the higher vibrations that come to you. Many shall cease their occupation with foolishness and will turn to the depth and the meaning of existence. Many will call upon Me for guidance and My Presence shall be with them in the midnight hour of coming events. When these events appear in a manner beyond their control, thoughts of My Sheep shall be turned towards My Words and spiritual Law. When the judgment hour is upon the planet, then shall the Shepherds consider and wonder if they also shall be weighed in the balance and found wanting.

7. There have been many warnings sent forth throughout My Father's Kingdom. There have been whisperings within hearts and there shall be a rushing to and fro when these things

begin to come to pass, as My Children seek to scurry into places of safety. I call My Children to move thyself within thy lands, away from the water, for much shall be cleansed from thy shores, by the washing of the waters. If ye believe MY Words, then ye will withdraw away from the waters that they will not overflow thee and thy dwelling.

Many winds will come, but My Children shall be warned. Listen ye for the still small voice within thy being, and be not hesitant to respond, but quicken thy understanding and get thyself up and away quickly.

8. Lay by in store for thyselves, thy supply, that ye be not found wanting in the days of crisis. Think ye that your world as ye know it, shall go on forever? I say unto thee, My Children, expect the unexpected and be ye prepared. Be ye wise as serpents and harmless as doves, that in these years of cleansing ye shall be found within the circle of My Love.

9. Times, and time and a half of time shall be thy endurance, and seven shall be the completion of the Day. Then shall ye know that stillness and peace have come, and deliverance hath come to the land. Then shall the birds of the air take flight again. Then shall the earth be stilled from its turmoil and then shall ye know that righteousness and joy shall inherit the Kingdom, and Love shall rise as the tide. Blessed are ye that shall inherit the earth, for behold I make a new earth, and ye shall be the inhabitants thereof. Ye shall go forth with singing and rejoicing that the end of thy tribulations hath come.

Then shall I walk beside thee. Then shall My Words be with thee, and My breath shall be in thy ear. The world will be filled with gladness and harmony, and each shall turn to help his neighbor and all that one hath shall be shared with another and none shall know need or want in My Father's Kingdom.

The darkness of the storm is but for a moment of time that the land may be bathed in freshness and newness once again. Then the sun rises upon it in splendor revealing its true beauty. Thus the earth will become green and clean again. The air shall be pure and wholesome. The spirit of men shall be mellowed and loving and life will explore new advancements for the good of all, and every soul shall know that I have been with them to deliver them.

They shall rub shoulders with those whom they have called the "angels," yet whom they have come to know as brothers from other worlds. The blessings of interdimensional fellowship, and interplanetary coexistence will lead the earth into heights of glory so long prepared for it. Nothing shall neither hurt nor destroy in all of the Kingdom. Mastery shall be over one's soul, and not over thy brother. Through great releases of incoming knowledge and new discoveries, all sickness shall pass away. The young shall grow freely, without fear of defilement, and the law shall be written in human hearts. Great shall be the brightness of My Father's Kingdom. His Grace is sufficient for thee to prepare to enter therein.

**I Am ESU, known to earth as**
**Jesus The Christ**

## Points to Ponder
### –or–
### (Group Discussion)

I. Souls have Celestial names (Esu), solar system names (Sananda) and (many) planetary names (Jesus).

2. His parting words were, "Feed My Sheep."

3. The spiritual temple not made with hands.

4. The integration of all Creation through the Christ Presence.

5. Reality *vs.* illusion.

6. The greatest revival in history.

7. Shorelines unsafe areas.

8. Survival preparations necessary.

9. The stillness that follows the storm.

## NOTES:

# 11:00AM—The Third Day
# Time Can Wait No Longer

## by NADA

Good morning, Tuella. I AM Mother Mary. I have come in this morning to bring you one who has served so well on the feminine ray in My Name. I come to introduce Ascended Lady Master Nada for her morning appointment. She has not spoken with you before, and I am very happy to bring you together. Beloved Lady Master Nada is very well informed, very dedicated and very alert to the times that are approaching. She speaks with you now:

"1. Greetings, my sister. I greet you in the Name of the Great I Am Presence within us all. I am Nada, and I know that you have followed the words of the Ascended Masters for many years. It is all on the record, you know. Every moment spent listening to their words, in person, in meditation, on tape or in print, or even calling their names; all of these things are recorded within the energy field which responds to those vibrations and absorbs the Light from the Ascended Ones.

2. I am delighted to contribute to these messages. This is a very crucial decade, a time when guidance is greatly needed. There cannot be too much of it released to the souls who struggle with their decisions. There is a fear abroad in the land. Perhaps on outer levels it would seem that pleasure and worldly pursuits have the upper hand, but one cannot rightly discern

from these. Within the hearts of thousands and thousands of persons, there is a gradual awakening and an acceptance of the fact that the world stands upon the threshold of great change. There is a trend towards a "buckling down" kind of attitude that prevails, and this is commendable. Where there has been a preoccupation with play, and fun and games, now humanity must grow up.

3. As we view the world panorama from our vantage point, it is naturally a sorrowing sight to see present conditions throughout the planet. All of life, and nature groans under the pressure of the weight of negativity and destructive thought forms. We would contain the results of these penetrations and dark emanations if that were possible. We do coordinate Divine Plans to ease the burden of planetary change as much as is possible under Universal Law. But in these times which signal the end of things as they have been, we are limited in the depth of our intervention. For there is a cleansing taking place as almost everyone is aware, and this is scheduled to come to pass. It MUST come to pass, and even now lags far behind the ordained time table. The world has not kept pace with the hopes and the plans of the Hierarchy, for its evolution and its transition into the higher frequencies for the coming Age.

Time can wait no longer! The Galaxy must continue on its given pathway. Time cannot stand still while mankind dawdles on his upward spiral. Humanity must pace itself to the times of the Age. The time is NOW for finding the pathway, completing the preparations, and donning the protection of Light for the changes that must come.

4. There is a great movement within the very bowels of the earth, that slowly rolls and rumbles and murmurs its coming threat. The planet cannot escape its murmurs within, but by the help of the heavenly forces and many helpers that serve the Light, much gentling can be given in this transition which lays aside the old and puts on the new. Many Beings and many Great Ones have come great distances to assist the Solar and

Planetary Hierarchies in the challenge of the coming decade. There will be sweeping changes in the very face of the land and the shape of the bodies of water.

There will be changes in the lifestyles because of prudent necessity. There will be changes in the thinking and mental levels of humanity. For coming in with the great scope of physical changes, will be the sweeping tides of change in attitudes toward the simplicities of life and the things that are vital. Those who have until now been detrimental to the advancement of Light, and continue in that frame of mind, will no longer be present to compete with that Light. Their adjustments to the uplifting of all life will not be possible, and they will be removed in one manner or another. The remnant will find harmony and cooperation advancing smoothly and suddenly it will seem that Brotherhood exists upon the earth once again, as souls are freed by the cleansing of the atmospheres, to expand the good that is inherent within every heart.

5 & 6. We of the Great Karmic Board, are jointly extending great mercy and great latitude during the decade to come. Great leniency will be the mood of the tribunal, as we serve in these coming days. Those who "will" to do the good, will find the good within them and the ability to do. I would speak directly to those who struggle to keep afloat in throes of financial disorder and economic chaos, and those who strive so valiantly to lead their children into right paths, and those who serve in the Armies of Light; to all of these who struggle against great odds in their personal battles, I say to you, help is on the way!

The great incoming rays will strengthen you in all of these efforts and bring results undreamed of, if you will address your calls to the Great Karmic Board of heaven. Through the cleansing of the earth, and the manifested assistance of the heavenly host and the beams of Light, the sons and daughters of God can rise to their dominion over the trials of this transition.

Those who have walked with God and sought His Will,

whatever your earthly religion may be; if you desire His Light to shine upon you, your calls will be answered. The world around you may experience great unpleasantness and sufferings in the coming world changes; nevertheless, those who have looked heavenward for their sustenance and their security, shall not fall. If necessary, you shall literally be lifted up into the heavens away from it all, and the world will not even know that you are gone. If that is not necessary, you shall be overshadowed by the Presence of those who represent the Hierarchy of heaven, dedicated to your protection and your survival.

Let not fear be found within you, but look to the heavens from whence cometh your help. I pledge to you that all who read my words shall be sheltered beneath the everlasting arms of God's Love.

**I Am,**
**Nada**

## Points to Ponder
### –or–
### (Group Discussion)

I. The absorption of Light from celestial contacts.
2. Serious reflection changes nebulous attitudes.
3. The contagious contamination of astral effluvia.
4. Geological disasters gentled by Space Ship activities.
5. The armor within.
6. The struggle to exist in modern society.
7. Dominion over the trials of life is the birthright of God's children.

## NOTES:

# 3:00 PM—The Third Day
# A Planet in Peril

## by Lady Master Rowena

Good afternoon, Tuella. It is nice to speak with you again. I see that the messages are progressing beautifully and soon all of the material will be in hand. As you are aware, on earth I was known as Evangeline Adams, a master of astrology. I understand that your sponsor has given a suggested deadline for compiling your manuscript. I would enlarge on that with the emphasis that your astrological influences are at their finest if you can work close to the deadline given, with very helpful effects from now through that time, benefitting your outreach with favorable results.

I am sure that many persons have considered that in just a few months the world will only be one year away from 1982. This is a tremendous fact for contemplation. As the planets progress, following their paths across the heavens, every soul is affected by these influences and the rays which are administered through them by the Great Lords.

3. There are extraordinary conjunctions coming into sway in 1981 which will intensely influence all of life internationally. The various conjunctions of Saturn and Jupiter housed in Libra, upon three separate occasions, is a visitation of great import. This scourge of conjunctions in the house of Libra, combined with the accompanying eclipses, bring a great

50

balancing to the planet. A balancing action implies that the high shall be brought low and the low shall be raised higher. Whether we apply this thought on spiritual levels or physical levels, that balancing will come. The prevailing force-fields at the meeting of these two provocative planetary influences will have a greater depth of emphasis with the intensity of the coming eclipses and the infiltration of great rays beyond the solar system.

1980 has been a comparatively quiet year when we consider the year immediately ahead. The zenith of this assemblage will usher in great change upon the planet, beginning in 1981 and building until the end of 1982. Changes of all kinds will appear—changes of philosophy, chaotic changes in social environments, changes in religious concepts, changes in the economic stability of the world, and grave physical changes as the decade builds momentum. These will ultimately be changes for the better; changes that are a part of the ideological cleansing as well as a physical cleansing for the planet. There will be an unprecedented loss of life from natural causes, related to the activity of Jupiter and the eleven year cycle of sunspot activity. The nature kingdom will respond to these radiations, as hordes of insect life appear in inordinate quantities. 1981 will not be an easy year. It will bring many challenges that must be faced and many emergencies with which humanity must cope to the best of its ability.

5. As the great incoming external rays ever increase in a gradual way, and the release of higher energies are lowered into the earth atmosphere, there will be explosions of impatience and a lack of control in human behavior. Beware of these reactions, be not taken by surprise, but maintain your peace and mastery of the emotional life through all of the unexpected events.

With every passing day, the mass of the solar system gradually is shifting, bringing the planets nearer to one another to take up their positions of alignment in opposition to the earth

51

from the other side of the great sun. The peak of the results from this tremendous array in the skies, whatever they may be, will come into full force in late 1982. In that year and the two following, all past records of weather performance will have little value, for you cannot predict in a situation that has not occurred since records began. Weather that has been common to one area will appear in another; that which has been accustomed in one section of the nation shall disappear from that section and appear in another. Winters could become the most devastating in history with unprecedented long periods of freezing. Where there has been the usual date for the beginning of winter, there may be the remaining of summer. Where snow and ice have been unknown, they may paralyze unprepared localities. Wind will reverse its patterns in unpredictable manner and velocity. Where occasional electric storms have been mild, they could become torrents of fury. Your weather will not follow any recognizable pattern of trends of the past.

Be prepared for the unexpected. You have had a glimpse of radical departure from the norm in the unprecedented and widespread stagnated heat wave of this summer of 1980. Yet all of its severity was combined with unprecedented cool waves in other areas simultaneously. Human life is oriented to the weather in its need for survival. Changing weather performances, when drastic in nature, can create much suffering and loss.

This apocalyptic pattern in the heavens could initiate phenomena in the skies undreamed of in human experience. The potency of the combined magnetic pull of the aligned planets, will produce effects upon earth's force-field which can scarcely be conceived. And one must add to this potency the additional sortie of conjunctions of extraordinary nature intensified by the seven eclipses in 1982 and the powerful outside rays from the Great Central Sun outside this system. These are the focus of the concerted alert presently in effect throughout the fleets of the Guardians of the planet. The heavens are God's Divine calendar and they mark out His Days.

Many problems that involve the crust of the earth can be lessened and manipulated by the intervention of our beloved Space Friends. But with all of their broad technology and abilities, they cannot interfere with the orbit of the planets! During the three years that follow, the Guardians will lower their positions closer into your atmosphere to be of help to earth in any emergency.

When any evidence of hostility or warring activities on international levels comes to your attention, as a concerned CITIZEN OF THE UNIVERSE, you must make your voice heard in protest of this aggressive attitude. For the possibility involved in combining war maneuvers with the effects of astrological indications and the planetary alignment, could trigger massive earthquakes global-wide, and total annihilation. The dark planet of Shan is not a peaceful one, but all souls surely seek survival. The signs in the heavens could very well indicate there will be no place left to run to.

The aligning planets reach their crisis position, then gradually subside. It would appear that the crisis time will be passed by 1984 and 1985, as the earth begins its renewal. Planetary karma and the closing of this Age is written in the heavens. Expect the unexpected. Be alert and be prepared. Know that the very hairs of your head are numbered, and not even a sparrow can fall to the ground without the Heavenly Father. The Heavenly Father keepeth watch over His own. Hold fast to thy crown until these calamities be passed. He giveth His angels charge over thee to keep thee in all thy ways.

I Am,
Lady Master Rowena

## Points to Ponder
### –or–
## (Group Discussion)

I. 1981 midpoint of seven year alignment.
2. 1981–Uranus in 120° aspect to Sun as it crosses Vernal Equinox; Jupiter/Saturn conjunction in Libra 1/1, 3/3, 7/24; 1982–Rare Saturn/Pluto conjunction (every 33 years); Full planetary alignment, end of cusp beginning Age of Aquarius.
3. Eclipses: 3/1981 in Cancer, 7 in 1982.
4. Relationship of astrological patterns to world karma (Saturn brings karma).
5. Planets influence, but do not compel, human behavior, and challenging growth.
6. Weather performance during alignment.

### NOTES:

# 7:00 PM—The Third Day
# The Flow of Wisdom

### by Hermes

Good evening, friend of the Light. I have come to keep my promise at the appointed time. My name is Hermes, I am a Master and Teacher of Universal Wisdom. I am your speaker for the evening.

You have known of me and studied my principles. It has been my function to bring the hidden wisdom to Light, upon the planet. The principles I brought to earth are the foundation of the Ancient Wisdom in all the Mystery Schools since the beginning of time. It has been my privilege in many cultures to teach the ancient secrets of the unfoldment of the soul of man. These secrets have been recorded in the religions of the world. My teachings have been adopted in many ways and presented from many positions by great world teachers. But basically, all of the important bodies of wisdom literatures that follow truth are based upon the principles of Hermes. I am the Father of Truth and Understanding. It is the energy which I project into and through Universal Mind which leads to the quickening and enlightenment of the Thinker within you. Humanity now comes to this crucial hour when the divine wisdom shall flow like a river. When every living soul that abides upon the new earth shall desire the knowledge that comes from on high. I am Hermes, and I will be pouring Love and Wisdom into the

55

understanding of mankind, through the rays that are contributing to this transition.

The teaching of Light that has been gradually released into the lower octaves of earth, has contributed to all the good things that have advanced life upon the planet. For as a man thinketh in his heart, so is he. Wisdom is like that candle that a man lighteth and set upon a bushel, and it giveth Light to all in the house. Wisdom is a divine attribute of the triune being. It is that portion of inheritance in the manifestation of the Heavenly Father through His Creation. Wisdom shall unfold as the rose, and from this moment on, each petal shall gradually unfold in a gentle way that will lead to beauty and maturity within the souls of men.

We are inaugurating new schools of Universal Wisdom and expending our energies for the input of the teachings. The great Light which once was only to be found in the secret rooms and the secret orders shall now be shouted from the housetops. Man shall come to understand the divine philosophies and the majestic principles that will lead him to a knowledge of his inner being and his Godself.

The ancient teachings have progressed down through the centuries, with continuing releases of Light through chosen ones. But this has been as the pace of the snail in comparison to that which is to come. In these days, and this decade, the principles of Hermes shall be incorporated into every walk of life, as the earth steps forth into its new era of revelation and understanding.

It is a paradox that the grip of confusion within minds of men has been such that the darkness has been exalted as the way of Light, and the way of Light and self-understanding has been relegated to the darkness. Such is the confusion that has reigned throughout the ages. In the new order of things, your teachers will not be found in the fine robes upon the rostrum of ecclesiastica, but your great teachers shall be found in all walks of life, in the humble pathway, in the small groups of seekers, in the byways and the quiet places of life. My energies shall project wisdom and enlightenment to all whose hearts and minds are open to an affinity with Universal Mind. Humble unschooled hearts shall drink from the fountains of heavenly wisdom and drink from them fully.

Each man shall become a priest unto his own household. This is the day that separates the false from the true. Look not to the credentials of men and the authorities of those who rule over them. But seek ye the flow and wisdom and truth wherever it may be found, within, or without. The day of separation of priesthood and laity is gone forever, washed downstream in the pulsating rising tide of awareness and the vibrations of a new dispensation. Look not to the exalting of men, that would rule over that which God shall reveal to thee in the secret place. But rather, follow after truth as it has been given to thee by thy Godself within. Find the great freedom to receive, freedom to learn, freedom to know, freedom to understand, freedom to absorb, to enjoy the heavenly breezes of divine truth blowing through the open doors of your mind. The relentless flow of Universal Wisdom by my impetus shall come to all. Do not fear to separate yourself from those who do not choose to walk with truth. Leave them behind, in their painted sepulchers filled with dead men's bones. Turn your face toward the fresh blessing of personal revelation. I, Hermes, will lead you and bring to you kindred souls in the brotherhood of Wisdom.

This transition also brings its time of unpleasantness with difficult physical disturbances and environmental adjustments. But throughout any personal struggles you will have a kind of guidance you have never experienced before, because you have pursued the pathway of wisdom and truth. As the planet ascends into higher vibrations of Light, those of you who have occupied your thinking with the great philosophies built upon the Hermetic Principles, will ascend also into those octaves of growth and spiritual blessing.

My closing words are designed to give courage to those

who read. Fear not for the changes that come, for they bring with them spiritual knowledge and wisdom and understanding that are as yet undreamed of in the mind of humanity. I leave with you my benediction of wisdom and Light.

**I Am,**
**Hermes**

## Points to Ponder
### –or–
## (Group Discussion)
*(The principles of Hermes are here reprinted for your convenience)*

# The Seven Laws of the Hermetic Philosophy

I. The principal of mentalism. ALL IS MIND, THE UNIVERSE IS MENTAL. This principle explains the true nature of energy, power and matter.

2. The principle of correspondence. AS ABOVE, SO BELOW; AS BELOW, SO ABOVE. This principle enables man to reason intelligently from the known to the unknown.

3. The principle of vibration. NOTHING RESTS; EVERYTHING MOVES; EVERYTHING VIBRATES. This principle explains that the difference between manifestations of matter, energy, mind, and Spirit result from varying rates of vibration.

4. The principle of polarity. ALL IS DUALITY. EVERYTHING HAS POLES; EVERYTHING HAS ITS PAIRS OF OPPOSITES; LIKE AND UNLIKE ARE THE SAME. Opposites are identical but different in degree. Opposites are only two extremes of the same thing, with many varying degrees between.

5. THE UNIVERSE IS RHYTHM. Everything flows out, and in; everything has its tides; all things rise and fall. The pendulum swing manifests in everything, rhythm compensates. This principle of neutralization applies in affairs of the Universe, suns, worlds; in life, mind, energy, matter. There is always an action and a reaction, an advance and a retreat.

6. The principle of causation. EVERY CAUSE HAS

ITS EFFECT; EVERY EFFECT HAS ITS CAUSE; EVERYTHING HAPPENS ACCORDING TO LAW. CHANCE IS BUT A NAME FOR LAW NOT REC- OGNIZED. THERE ARE MANY PLANES OF CAU- SATION, BUT NOTHING ESCAPES THE LAW.

7. The principle of Gender. Gender is in every- thing, everything has its masculine and fem- inine principles. Gender manifests on all planetary levels. Every thing or person, con- tains the two principles within it, him or her.

–From THE KYBALION

"The lips of wisdom are closed, except to the ears of understanding.

# 7:00 AM—The Fourth Day
# Health in the New Age

### by Zoser

Hello again, Tuella. This is Zoser returning as promised and very anxious to speak with you once more. I enjoyed our last brief conversation and I have not forgotten you or your work for the Brotherhood. I am a Master of Healing, a teacher of healing and pyramidology. For I was the first builder of the Pyramid in your dimension.

1 & 2. I have come to speak regarding the healing art and technique, particularly the innovations that will contribute to "HEALTH IN THE NEW AGE." We are entering an entirely different era in the science of healing. The cycle just ending has been predominantly the day of surgery and the dispensing of drugs on a frightening scale. In the awakening that is at the very door, electronics will be the primary tool of the healing practitioner. Science will awaken to the electronic field as it applies to diagnosing the human aura. Research in this field under the sponsorship of the guiding Guardians, from the higher Archives of Wisdom, will lead to the introduction of diagnostic devices of this nature. The New Age physician will need to become familiar with these devices. In the New Age, instruments will be in use, with which the medical person can

diagnose the human aura by scanning it with the sensitive instrument, somewhat similar in appearance to the remote control device used with your television sets. The sensitive equipment will absorb the currents within the human aura and register them on a graph, literally drawing a picture for the healer. A large screen will show the outline of the human form, and as the auric scanning proceeds, electronic sketches will appear upon the screen. Where weakness prevails, or disease is present in any portion of the anatomy, disharmony of any kind will be located on the screen sketch. This, then, is the new direction for diagnostic procedures.

3. Proceeding from diagnosis to treatment, the New Age physician will then turn to another newly projected piece of electronic equipment. The auric penetrating equipment will beam a force-field of healing ray to that area in need of balance as indicated. Healing will take place in the physical form as the electronic beam is administered through the electromagnetic field of the body of the patient, the treatment being administered to the identical spot in the human auric field.

4. Preventative healing technique will come forth through the perfecting of further electronic equipment designed to "charge" the physical energy field, the magnetism, the metabolism of the body. This machine will literally withdraw from the atmosphere the atomic energy particles and assimilate them in such a manner, that they may be redirected to the human form before it. This will represent a treatment in general well-being of a preventative nature.

5. The New Age will bring a tremendous sweep toward healing through nutrition, so lacking today in the medical hierarchies. A whole new phase of food study in depth, will occupy the minds researching this field. This occupation of course becomes a form of preventative healing also, but there will also be the treatment of imbalance by prescribing certain combinations of certain foods. This combination procedure is very technical; it will be widely used in the New Enlightenment, as

old methods deteriorate and new practices are instituted.

**6 & 7.** When the drugs of this day are laid aside and chemicals are removed from the daily diet, there will be an exhilarating step toward body balance, harmony and good health. The present revolution toward "health foods" is but a shadow of that which is to come on a broad scale. More and more, this will begin to displace the old patterns of the typical family menus. New educational programs will include guiding the children toward the new concepts in nutrition, from their first registration, and they will not be exposed to harmful foods within the schools. Here and there within the land, there is an awakening in this connection. Many schools today are attempting to institute more nourishing snack items and menus.

**6.** So many of the sweeping changes are slow in their inception because they represent a complete reeducation and reorientation of mental approach to so many problems that exist today. Healing and nutrition are not exceptions to this rule. It takes time to make the transition from present accepted methods in these later centuries and move into the electronic age of healing.

This is especially true in disorders of the brain. The new electronic fact-finding, diagnostic equipment shall be especially helpful for these disorders. There will also prevail an understanding and realization that as a man thinketh, so will his thoughts be reflected in physical manifestation. In time, the physicians will take into consideration the entire being of the patient, and all four of his lower bodies, as parts of his united whole, in every diagnosis and treatment.

**7.** I am Zoser, a master of healing and a physician of long ago. I have been a master of these things for many civilizations and have myself been a physician on earth many times. I also foresee once again, the use of precious minerals and gems in the administration of the healing arts. This was once widely practiced and has suffered ill repute down through the various cultures. But mankind will once again begin to discern the great life-giving properties, and the energies of the minerals and the precious gems and the manner in which they may be used to tone the physical form.

8. As souls enter deeper into the entire environment of a new earth, and a new life, more and more, sickness and illness will be phased out of human experience. For the spiritual quality of life itself, the positiveness of the thought level, the effect of the act of loving all souls, will be evidenced in the gradual disappearance of disharmony, imbalance and poor health. Positive mental attitudes, calmness, serenity, mastery of the emotional life, balanced physical experiences, will ultimately bring forth perfection of the physical form. This will be a great day for evolved humanity, when they may stand in the wholeness and the perfection, and the purity of the balanced life.

I send my blessings of wholeness and Love and Light to each and everyone.

I Am,
Zoser

## Points to Ponder
## –or–
## (Group Discussion)

1. A.M.A.'s careless use of surgery and drugs.
2. Diagnosing through the human aura.
3. Healing administered through the human aura.
4. Charging the energy field as a form of preventative healing.
5. Healing through the new nutrition.
6. The electronic age of healing.
7. The use of gems in healing.
8. The ultimate perfection of the human form.

### God's Universal Family

God has a large family
Extending far and wide,
No limits or boundaries
Will ever stop
The onrushing tide
Of the love of God's creatures
In His family of One,
And His Kingdom so vast;
Bound together by love
That forever will last.

—Eileen Schoen

# 11:00 AM—
# The Fourth Day
# Science in the New Age

### by Melchior

**1.** I am Melchior, a Master of Alchemy and Science. I have served humanity in being instrumental in presenting to the planet many new discoveries. This is my field. It is my work to constantly survey new avenues of approach to science which is for the benefit of mankind.

**2.** I have come to you with the permission of Lord Kuthumi, to speak concerning the position of science in its relationship to the New World, which will be operative when the New Age is underway. We have been withholding many wonderful discoveries for mankind, because your scientific community has not been conducive to the kind of inspiration that would bring these blessings to your world. You see, Tuella, there are many wonderful revelations waiting in the shadows for manifestation when the mind of man has been cleansed and acclimated to the New Age environment.

I could describe dozens and dozens of tremendous advancements that are at the very doors of the world laboratories. Nevertheless, these must be withheld until mankind is worthy to receive them. The nature of some would allow them to be perverted toward negative purposes, and we of the Broth-

erhood may not risk their release under present world conditions. Revelations within the medical field which would wipe
out many present diseases are necessarily withheld, because of
the commercialization and manipulation which would take
place. These and many other blessings must wait for a better
day to come.

3. In the meantime, may I address your scientific world
and appeal to the great minds of research, to release all personal desires for notoriety and gain, and yield yourselves as
dedicated servants to the betterment of humanity. The time is
so short, time is so brief for these endeavors, that I would project the call that the men of great mental stature would surren-
der their personal goals for the greater goals of humanity,
striving forward into the new vibrations as they enfold the
planet. The modern facilities of science have adequate equipment to pursue holistic avenues of thought. Thousands of
untrodden paths of investigation are waiting for the dedicated
humanitarian souls of the scientific arena. There are untold
answers to be given for problems to be solved, when the inner
creativity blends with spiritual intuition, to fire the imagination
and inspire assistance from Higher Realms. For in the final
analysis, all discovery lies hidden within the Universal Mind.

4 & 5. I call upon the scientists, yeah, I challenge them, to
meditate at great length, and to seek the inspired thought and
the whispered direction that comes from the voice of Divinity
within. Here lies the navigation of uncharted seas of revelation,
awaiting that one who dares to pit himself along with the great
Ones of Higher Worlds, who stand ready to cooperate in ven-
tures into the unknown. Let science push back the horizon of
their conceived possibilities, and practice open-mindedness
toward spiritual infiltration of ideas born of spiritual wisdom.
For truly this is as much a part of the purity of inspiration as is
any great symphony or lyric in verse. Inspiration takes many
forms, but has but One Source, the Divine Mind. Muse upon
your problems in the silence and the solitude of the secret place

of the Most High, and in quietness and confidence await your inspiration and solution. Let the Divine Light shine upon your mental activities, for within the Mind of God all things are born and brought into manifestation. Divine creativity and genius are the inherent possibilities of every soul. Genius is a heavenly attribute. It cannot be attained within your halls of learning. It is a flaming fire endowed from on high, upon those who have not chosen it, but have been given it as a gift of God. So, let that which comes from above, return to that which is above and seek its fulfillment from its original Source.

There is an Edison or an Einstein hidden within every student of science waiting to be brought forth into manifestation. I challenge the scientists of this day, to dare to open their minds to the expansion in the Light and spiritual intuition from other worlds. Only in this manner may the releases be permitted which they have sought for so long. Humanitarian interest must prevail and overcome the pursuit of mammon in your world.

6. These generations are infiltrated with those of other worlds who have come to become a part of your scientific society in order to bring into it the releases under Hierarchal Plans. They are hidden in your laboratories everywhere. They serve in humility in an unknown place, under the inspiration of the Higher Ones. When a cleansing of the attitude of your scientific world takes place, these chosen ones will begin to bring forth these benefits and blessings which are due to come. These shall be spared in troublesome times, and their labors shall be a part of the great reconstruction of life upon the planet. They shall contribute to the great unfolding of scientific revelation that will launch the New Age. I speak to these young scientists, whose desire is a sincere devotion to the needs of mankind. I say to these, I encourage you to stand silently in your place, until the secret inspirations of your quiet times can be revealed and manifested. Your day will come. Your mission shall be fulfilled.

I Am,
Melchior

## Points to Ponder
### –or–
### (Group Discussion)

I. Scientific advancement is released from higher realms.
2. These releases are conditional.
3. Spiritual dedication necessary within the scientific community.
4. Spiritual awareness.
5. The source of genius.
6. There are chosen ones in every field of human endeavor.

## NOTES:

# 3:00 PM—The Fourth Day Tribute to Woman

### by Ascended Lady Master Venus

Good evening, my sister. I greet you in the Light of the Beloved. I am Lady Master Venus. I am the Divine Complement of Sanat Kumara, Lord of our planet. I come to you from Venus and bring you our radiation of Love and Blessings. I have been invited by Beloved Lord Kuthumi to participate in this effort in sending forth his volume foursquare. I therefore pour my energies into it, to blend with his and all of those who speak, in preparing a vortex of Light to be lowered into manifestation at this time. I release with my words, the energy from our planet to bring Love and Light into manifestation within the souls of mankind.

1 & 2. At this hour, I bring to the women of the planet earth, my special touch from the higher octaves of Venus. I breathe upon womankind the divine courage and strength that will be needed by them in the coming decade of destiny. For it seems that in the darkest hours of testings and troubles, woman is lifted and exalted in her assistance as comforter. The special gentleness of motherhood and companionship is magnified in times of stress, and the tenderness that proceeds forth from their own indwelling faith, is poured out on those in their

circle of blessing. The children and the fathers look to the mothers for that special kind of divine guidance that never fails to appear when it is needed. I shed a special dispensation of Love and Serenity upon the women of the earth, to guide and support them as they support others when support is most needed. Hearts who call upon the Reality beyond temporal things to find the answers to life shall receive a beam from my own Being, a faith that shall sustain these Beings of Light, as they become pillars of strength in the coming decade.

3. Many shall be the problems that beset your world which we would sweep away completely if that were possible. But all are aware that you progress forward, inexorably marching toward your great fulfillment. All of the solar system must progress in its pathway and changes must come, and have come to other planets as well as yours. Yet all must progress as one, and none may lag behind or hinder another. Thus it is that progression must come to beloved Terra and changes will bring you your glory. The solar system may then move on in its pathway of Light.

4. Let the women gather the children around them and explain with words of Love when these things are upon you, that Love is manifesting to bring a greater world and a New Age for their sakes and their leadership. Strengthen the faith of your men. Gently expose their hearts to the reality of other worlds and the angelic host.

So often the men of your planet do not have the available time or lengthy opportunities to pursue spiritual investigation. But a loving companion who can find the time may absorb new revelation and share it in quiet moments. Thus that one who must leave the home and go forth to a day filled with pressures of materialistic nature can be spiritually lifted in the quiet moments with his loving companion in the home environment.

5. Your world progresses in its daily affairs within such clutter and haste that truly there is little time for spiritual refreshment. So much of womankind must now also go forth

into the stream of materialism in the workaday world. Yet the soul of woman is by nature inclined toward the softness of heart and the gentleness of Love and an intuitive knowing of that which is right. So that even as woman is placed outside the home environment and surrounded in the kingdom of mammon, she can, even there, radiate her subtle influence for balance to permeate the rigid atmospheres of negativity.

6. Take care that the circumstances and necessities of life do not overwhelm your feminine heritage. You are woman, and as such you are a beautiful channel for the implementation of divinity in your world. The nature of your calling and responsibilities as a woman endow your inner being with an exultation of awareness. The Christ Consciousness finds an easy expression in the gentleness of woman.

As you approach a crisis in planetary evolution, the women of the world will be called upon to be towers of strength and quietness. Now is the time to prepare the inner citadel by magnetizing to yourself a greater faith, a closer attunement with the Higher Ones, a deeper devotion to the Heavenly Father. For the challenges that are before you will require a spiritual stamina that is the fruit of consistent application of spiritual law.

Women will need to be the hands and the voice of Christ within their households. As the mothers of the world prepare to lay by for their families stores of food and necessities and supply, as guidance has been given, I would pray that she would also lay by in the storehouse of the inner being, more faith and blessings. The secret closet of prayer, neglected because of the press of things, must be restored as a ritual of vital import, and faithfully maintained. The prayers of woman for her family can build a force-field of power around the home into which the angels of God can descend and ascend in administering their protection. Build a force-field of Light around your individual world by your calls heavenward, and I will respond with my Presence and blend my vibrations with those of woman in that hour.

I send to all women who handle this little book, my emanations of strength and love.

I Am,
**Lady Master Venus**

## Points to Ponder
### –or–
### (Group Discussion)

I. The coming decade will require a special degree of spiritual strength.
2. The feminine ray as comforter.
3. Changes unavoidable for the world.
4. Woman as the family teacher.
5. The feminine ray in the world.
6. Fortify the inner citadel.

### Night Cry

If ever you hear a soft sob in the night,
It's a mother and wife bursting with fright;
At the horrors of war—and its sly machinations,
That bring death and destruction
To large and small nations.

She gave of the love of her heart, oh so true,
The mate of her soul, the more for to rue;
And later as time repeats errors unsolved,
She gave of her sons, but no more to resolve
The conflicts of men.

For the war machine swallows them up
With mercy denied, leaving nothing but horror
With death it remains forever allied
So whenever you hear a sob in the night,
Send mercy and prayer and God-filled Light.

—Eileen Schoen

# Section Three
# World Guardians

## The Coming of the Guardians

While the world appears to crumble
Some are frantic, crazed with fear—
Become at last, meek and humble,
Certain now, end times are here.
As harlequins they have existed
Pantomiming patterns of destruction;
Living, breathing, false illusions!
Why must it take a crisis
For souls to share
And trust, and help each other
Through times of history so rare?

Yet, trusting ones, have naught to fear
They've readied for this final scene,
And in God's Plan for earth's new birth
Have placed their trust in Him, unseen.
But right or wrong it makes no difference
For all are one in His Dear Sight.
And coming soon is their deliverance
But first—His messengers of Light
Will come from other galaxies
In deep concern for earth's dire plight.

Think you that your earth can fall
While brother, sister worlds stand idly by?
The word goes forth—you shall not perish
For don't you know that
Stars and planets and other worlds
Are all of God—His own to cherish?
Eons ago they learned His laws,
And of their own volition do obey;
Thus, if a sister planet stumbles
Errs and goes astray,
They stand alert—and ready

76

To assist earth's family.

With wisdom that ye know not of
Millions, are your friends above.
Be not afraid of other humans
From His planets great and holy,
But welcome these dedicated ones
As part of the Creator's family
Of many precious God-wrought Sons.

—Eileen Schoen

# 7:00 PM The Fourth Day Ashtar Command Communique

The Ashtar Command is present overhead everywhere upon the planet. There are thousands and thousands of ships in our many fleets that make up the Ashtar Command. We are the Etherians, and ours is the authority that controls the entire Space Program for the planet.

We have stated that mankind is responsible to himself to search out his weaknesses and to call upon the Higher Ones for strength to change for the better. Man is Master of his fate and Captain of his soul. He is accountable for all the great releases of Light that have been given to the planet century after century and civilization after civilization.

We have endured the ridicule and the foolishness of your media with long-suffering and patience. We have endured while our representatives and those whom we have contacted have been swayed from their convictions by the eloquence of your federal officials. There have been times when we have been amazed that this could take place, but this is the way of your planet. In the coming decade there will be signs in the heavens that your glib talking officials will be unable to deny. For an awakening has come at last to the population of the planet and an awareness of the purpose of help of a high order coming to mankind, ever closer and closer, every day that passes.

We of the Ashtar Command would speak to your world leaders and the spokesmen of your great assemblies, and CHALLENGE them to trust our words and believe in our presence and begin to accept the help which we bring to your world. The worldwide problems that beset your United Nations on every hand, can be solved in the unity and cooperation of your people with your friends and brothers from other worlds. This ostrich-like position that has prevailed in the last two decades can no longer stand the test of events that are about to come to pass. Once again we extend the hand of friendship and an offering to share our intelligence and research, our assistance in all of the programs that are underway for the benefit of humanity.

We only ask that you lay down your arms, that you lay aside your plans for nuclear destruction, that you cease to pervert the great discoveries of energies, and that you start to convert them for the benefit of all humanity. The Ashtar Command calls upon the military men of this planet to meet together in one place at one time and forge an agreement for worldwide peace, that is not false words upon paper but is the depth of feeling within the heart of every military statesman.

Because of your indifference and your ridicule to channel our words and our directives through the men and women of the land in an official capacity, our approach in an official way of many years ago was spurned by your global authorities.

Once again for a brief period, we extend to your President, the House of Representatives, the men of your Senate, and all of your national leaders, our hand of friendship and cooperation. In the Name of the salvation of the life of Humanity, we ask that you would receive our words and WELCOME US TO SPEAK IN YOUR ASSEMBLIES! WE HAVE THOSE WHO CAN WALK AMONG YOU AND NEVER BE

NOTICED FOR ALL THEIR SIMILARITY TO YOUR OWN APPEARANCE. THEY CAN SUDDENLY APPEAR BEHIND YOUR ROSTRUM AND SPEAK TO THE MEMBERS OF YOUR CONGRESS. WE WOULD PREFER TO BE INVITED TO DO THIS. IF WE ARE NOT INVITED TO DO THIS, WE MAY HAVE TO ARRANGE OUR OWN OPPORTUNITY TO SPEAK TO THESE GENTLEMEN, IN THE EARLY PART OF THIS DECADE. FOR THERE IS TOO MUCH AT STAKE ON A PLANETARY BASIS AS WELL AS INTER-PLANETARY REACTIONS TO STAND BY WITHOUT AN EFFORT TO PROBE THE MOTIVATIONS BEHIND PRE-SENT WORLD DISORDER.

We send this message as an advancing envoy and ask the world leaders and the governments of all the world to make a place for our spokesman upon your agendas.

*IF THE SPACE IS MADE, THE SPOKESMAN WILL APPEAR!*

This message is sent to planet earth by the members of the Ashtar Command.

PEACE ON EARTH! GOOD WILL TOWARD MEN!

• • •

*All copyright restrictions are hereby lifted from this Core-munique in the hope that it might have the largest circulation possible.*

*Spread copies to all of your government representatives, and all the addresses you know of United Nations officials and World Peace representatives.*

*Send Ashtar's plea to all the leaders of the nations, that all of the sons of God throughout the Universes would unite in an effort toward Universal Peace and Brotherhood.*

*-Tuella*

# 7:00 AM The Fifth Day
# We Are The Reaping Angels

## by Commander Soltec

Greetings in the Light of the Radiant One. I am Kadar-Monka, of the Saturn Tribunal. I bring to you on this beautiful morning my very good assistant in all of the Space Federation Programs. I introduce to you now Commander Soltec, Space Scientist and Sun Technician, whose vibrations have been within your force-field for many weeks. Together we have monitored your thoughts and Soltec has come to keep his appointment for your vigil. He now speaks:

Greetings to you, sister of Light. It is my pleasure to speak with you personally. I have been planning this encounter for quite some time, having been approached by the Great Lord Kuthumi to be one of the speakers of the forthcoming volume. I am grateful for this opportunity to speak to many souls. I consider the presentations of these messages to be very timely. The symposium of many speakers on the subject of the coming decade is certain to make an impact upon alerted souls.

1. We of the Space Federation have been working through our emissaries and messengers throughout this present century. Now we find that all of the past efforts are coming to focus in the eighties. Our encompassing participation in planetary

affairs has been extensive. There is scarcely an area of planetary life, in which our combined efforts have not participated. We have been active in the kingdom of nature and raising its vibrations, in penetrating its world to cleanse the very spirit of nature, which has been one of competitiveness and ruthlessness in its effort toward survival. A period of change is now operative in the vibrations that influence the planet and its entire force-field. We have been active in the higher atmospheres of your interplanetary activities and preventing your self-destruction at your own hand.

We have intervened in great weather disturbances, propelling our energy forces into situations that would have caused great destruction and loss of life. We have cast our beams upon the leaders of your world in an attempt to gentle the vibrations and the directions of their thinking. We have stood within the force-field of your great national and international bodies in their times of deliberation, attempting by the magnetism of our invisible presence to sway the decisions toward peace upon the earth. Our presence everywhere in all activities and situations has circumvented events to bring the world to this hour to face the challenges of the coming decade. Once again our presence surrounds you in a great radiant sphere of influence and projection that will cast out all fear and inspire the faith within you that is vital to your survival.

2. The emanations of the Great Light throughout planetary affairs is beginning to be recognized by those capable of this discernment. That which cannot enter the penetrations of Light must remain forever outside its domain. This would seem to contraindicate a strengthening of the darkness, but this is untrue. It is only a reaction of that which is the absence of the Light in its resistance to penetration of the Light. We foresee in the coming decade an unprecedented advancement in the fields of spiritual awareness to know scientific principles, because the scientific community will be overshadowed by heavy preponderances of Light that will open their minds to receive guidance

from the Higher Beings.

3. The incoming rays will enhance mental faculties to flow freely along spiritual lines. Advances in electronics will express these spiritual principles through much new equipment which will radically change life as it has been experienced in the past.

Interplanetary communication devices shall be perfected, finally answering the questions of many centuries. Electronics will invade the medical field, bringing with them once and for all the absolute concept of man as a spiritual being while within a physical form. Countless blessings are in store during and following the time we have come to call the cleansing of the planet.

All other cleansings have been completed. The interplanetary world, the astral world, the world of nature, are all nearing the completion of their preparations to enter the next dimension. Only the earth and its inhabitants remain to be prepared for this great transition into the new orbit of destiny. What is to be and what is to come is so glorious and so wonderful it is worth any price you may be called upon to pay.

4. We are present with you throughout your heavens. Though you may not see us as often as you like, our presence is nevertheless constantly overshadowing all of your world. We will be in continual orbit surrounding every portion of the globe, systematically registering all of your thoughts and your activities as well as rendering a guardian patrolling action of protection.

My good friend, Hatonn, will be discussing with you the qualifications for rescue as that proves necessary, so I will not elaborate upon that subject. I would simply wish to express for your understanding, the absolute certainty that you are not forsaken, that we are as close as your very breath, for your thoughts are registered with us upon our great monitoring board and equipment. Wherever a call or cry for help of any kind is projected heavenward by one of you, that call is immediately registered upon our equipment. Help is immediately projected within your force-field. Therefore, there is no justification for the presence of fear, in any situation that might befall your community, your area or your nation. For we are the listening angels, we are the reaping angels, who will see and hear the cry of your heart and help will be dispatched along the ray of your projection the very moment you have beamed it to us.

5. Your Space Friends are here at the request of the Most High Interplanetary Hierarchy, and the Great Cosmic Government. We are here to do their bidding. We have come in voluntary action to serve you, the people of earth, in your time of great distress. This is the message that I would leave with you, the fact of our presence. WHEREVER YOU ARE AT THIS VERY MOMENT, DIRECTLY OVER YOU, YOU ARE BEING OBSERVED AND MONITORED BY SOME REPRESENTATIVE OF OUR COOPERATIVE GUARDIAN ACTION. For these are crucial times. We cannot state with any certainty or give any specific dates when certain events will take place. But we are in an alert at all times, for any eventuality that may suddenly come upon you.

However, our primary ministry to the souls of earth, is to beam forth whatever assistance we may bring in your search for an inner awakening and awareness of Light. This we stand ready to do at the first indication that this is desired. As you pursue the Light YOU ARE NOT ALONE! Unimaginable help comes to you as you take the first step on the pathway of Light. Think of this coming decade as that period when an entire planetary body takes its step into a new pathway of Light.

I am your Brother, and a Commander in the forces of Light, the Light of the Radiant One. I salute you in His Matchless Name. Adonai Vasu Barragus.

—Soltec

## Points to Ponder
### –or–
### (Group Discussion)

I. The broad scope of Guardian Action.
2. Discernment of the incoming Light.
3. The electronic invasion.
4. Our world is overshadowed by their presence.
5. You are overshadowed by their Love.

## NOTES:

# 11:00 AM The Fifth Day The Unfolding of the New Light Bearers

## by Commander Korton

1. Good morning! I am here to speak as scheduled with the morning message. I come under the banner of Kuthumi. I am the Master of all Space Communications and coordinator of messages. I am Korton, and we have spoken together before. I am from KOR, the great communication center working from the planet Mars. All messages and space communications are relayed through our center, and from there they are beamed to our craft and on to your planet. I am a Commander in the Confederation and one who has monitored many messages which you have received from all of us. Prayers from the children of Light, as they rise heavenward, are monitored and relayed by those with me in this great communication system.

2. I am here this morning to report to you that many hundreds of fine new channels are opening to us and our frequencies, through the great rays that are beamed to the planet. Those sincere souls who have sought contact with us for a long period of time, shall be rewarded, for the enabling rays will bring expansion of spiritual expression and spiritual experience in all forms. The vibrations that arise and surround the planet have increased and risen so greatly in recent months that

all of heaven is rejoicing for that which has been accomplished in spiritual advancement. The ability of those whose service it is to bring enlightenment to the mass consciousness is greatly enhanced and speeding onward to accomplishment.

3. We are pleased to report that many of your youth are opening their being to the proper seeking of true Light. So many have been captivated by cults and influences of Luciferian forces parading as Light. So many young lives have been deceived, that the order from on High has gone forth for the penetration of Light to dissolve the strongholds of darkness and bring young hearts into the plateaus of pure Light. Much concentrated effort presently in action, is beamed toward your younger generation, that they may begin their ascension into Light and Understanding, for the leadership that will be given them in the days to come.

Many great ones with higher missions to humanity are presently scattered throughout your high schools and educational centers. These are known to us in a precious way, and their whereabouts and progress is carefully documented in our records in Space. We are in cooperation with the Planetary Hierarchy in keeping our beams upon these special souls, that their feet shall not slip from the pathway and that they may not be detoured from their destiny.

In love, we understand the sorrow that has come to many hearts because of the infiltration of the drug traffic into the lives of your children and the youth of the land. This sorrow extends throughout the Universes for this waste of human potential and waste of human creativity. We desire to report that action is and has been in motion to cleanse this blight in the lives of your coming generation.

4. Your crime syndicates, with all of their tentacles and various avenues of destructive activities, are placed and carried on by the endowment of energies from the dark forces who oppose us. But these energies have now been overruled and shall be withdrawn for they are a blasphemy when used to

destroy. The highest Council of Heaven has demanded the destruction of all plots and actions designed to corrupt the younger generation. This is a part of the divine program for cleansing the land.

In this coming decade you will see the manifestation of the withdrawal of the power of these energies and their clutch upon your children. For that which is the absence of Light shall be filled with the brightness of the Light of the Cosmic Rays NOW being shed upon humanity of all ages and all nations.

5. In Light groups and Light centers around the planet, preparations and plans must be made for teaching the children and the young people, the principles and the philosophies as given by all of the Great Masters of Light. Awareness comes very natural to the very young. These experiences are to be encouraged and expanded. For the children come with a capacity to grasp the inner teachings that has not been present upon earth for many cultures and eons of time. Do not block the unfoldment of your young people for it is their coming destiny, they cannot escape it. As the joy it brings transcends their earthly search for thrills and excitement, they will come to realize there is no thrill on earth to compare with the joy of a knowledge of the Inner Presence. This is the heritage of today's children. The pearl of great price which they must find, as they progress under the loving and watchful eye of your friends from outer space.

I salute everyone in the Light of the Radiant Adonai vassu Adonai. I Am,

—**Korton**

## Points to Ponder
### –or–
### (Group Discussion)

I. The great KOR communications center for the solar system.
2. The inevitable expansion of spiritual gifts.
3. Make way for the New Light Bearers.
4. Dark forces supply energies for all destructive activities.
5. Schools of Light for the young must come.

## NOTES:

# 3:00 PM The Fifth Day
# We Must Assume
# Responsibility

Matton speaking. I have come a great distance, through many galaxies, to keep my appointment with you this beautiful afternoon. I am the Space Master responsible for the coordination of all the Space Volunteers throughout the universe. I have been given this appointment by Kuthumi, and I speak as a representative of all of the Alliance and the entire Space Confederation.

1. We of the Volunteer Space Program to planet Earth have coordinated every effort and all of our energies toward these days. We have longed and dreamed to see that hour when Earth would qualify to become a member of its own Solar System. At long last that moment is about to come to pass, when Earth will voluntarily enter the Galactic Pact, and willingly assume the treaties and rules and that great document of Universal Peace. Earth must be willing to honor that commandment which states, "Thou shalt not kill," whether by war or any other cause. Then shall there be Peace throughout the firmament of the Heavenly Father.

2. We must assume some of the responsibility for the acts of your planet, for it was to you that we sent those disruptive

and rebellious units of consciousness when our heavens were cleansed of all warlike propensities. As the cleansing took place elsewhere, your planet became the recipient of these unworthy ones who were left to mingle with you, and to propagate within your society [*fugitives of Maldek—T.*]. We have all, therefore, joined our forces and offered our time and technology to finally rescue the beautiful planet of Earth from the hold of these malevolent forces of Lucifer, that rely upon death and destruction and bondage of humanity. That bondage shall be broken, for all men must be free! They must be loosed to follow the dictates of their own inner guidance and inner divine convictions for their lives and their world. Thus it has been that the wheat and the tares have been allowed to grow together, but now that harvest has come.

We of the Universal Confederation, Guardians of your planet, are the reaping angels who shall come to separate the chaff and to gather the wheat into the Father's storehouse. We of other worlds have accepted this responsibility to your planet and your people. Our service to the Radiant One has been long and steadfast and loyal. In my assignment as coordinator of this program, it has been my privilege to personally meet and become acquainted with untold thousands of shining souls, who have come to offer their help in this service to humanity in its difficult transition. These are souls with a dedication to the Heavenly Father, and an awareness of themselves as Light Beings of His Creation.

Many constellations, many galaxies, and even many other universes, are represented in this group that passes before me. This Alliance has strengthened and contributed to the bond of love between all of our worlds, as our hearts have united in this program of evolution for Earth and its people.

You are now well on the way and off to a good start. Light is expanding upon you and within you. The hold of the dark ones is loosening each day that passes, and the stars in their courses are leading you on to your fulfillment. Trust us, for we are your friends. We come in Love and dedication to this great cause which will unite all worlds in peace and brotherly love. We are standing by, organized, alerted and ready in the twinkling of an eye to serve you as brothers.

4. Yield yourselves as instruments of Light upon your planet and channels of peace. Let Love control your Being and Love penetrate all of your affairs. Only those who live in love for fellow man are numbered for fellowship with us. Recognize and realize the Presence of the Beloved Christ in every other human face, and honor that Christ within. When you think upon us, remember that each one of us who patrol your skies, is a manifestation of the Creator, even as you.

Do not let thoughts of approaching events overwhelm you. Instead, find your confidence and strength in the secret place of the Most High. Be still and know that the Father will never forsake you, when you put your trust in Him. We come to you as Brothers, in His Name. I am a Brother from other worlds.

I Am,
Matton

## Points to Ponder
### –or–
### (Group Discussion)

I. Earth must join the solar system in universal peace.
2. The fugitives from Maldek and the corruption of humanity.
3. The love and dedication of our Space Friends.
4. Brotherly Love is a prerequisite for interplanetary fellowship

## NOTES:

# 7:00 PM The Fifth Day
# The Aura of Urgency

## by Philip The Apostle

Good evening, Tuella. I am Philip the Apostle of Jesus Christ. I am coming to you in the planetary identity in the vibration of the memory of that lifetime which you shared with me as one of my daughters. Therefore I choose to come to you under that name, because of our link in that lifetime with Our Beloved Lord. I have come to participate in the messages that will be given to the world. I come in a sense of the *urgency* of the times.

1 & 2. I am compelled to use that word, for the time is short and the end draweth nigh, and in your generation you shall see the fulfillment of things long awaited. In my present position as a member of the Saturnian Council, I am well informed regarding planetary affairs. We are never without information that is current to the minute regarding the proposals of nations and their cabinet leaders and the plans for military action or non-action. I regret that the former is more prevalent than the latter. We watch with great concern, the great oil supplies and those that control them, in the various nations. We see much potential danger in connection with world oil supplies. We concern ourselves with the stand of

Israel and the Afghanistan invasion and the worldwide economy, for all of these things can build a momentum toward the loss of diplomatic interchange. These are crucial times. There is an urgency in our Council meetings and an alert throughout the interplanetary councils.

3. We are warned by the watchmen on the walls, of great deposits of nuclear weapons and dangerous blastings which jar the faultlines of the planet. We observe the manipulation of weather patterns and the hoarding of weapons and man's inhumanity to man. Mankind, in a very short time, will become occupied with survival from the onslaughts of nature. To multiply coming world problems with a plan for nuclear destruction is unthinkable. Yet there are those who are thinking of it at this very hour. We must watch these situations as one would watch the young toddler reaching for the matchbox. The aura of emergency surrounds our every thought.

The Great Tribunal of the Solar System has very few alternatives. This untimely linking of two potentials for global disaster is a grave concern of every member of our group. It is not enough to rely upon some far-off mass evacuation by the planetary Guardians. It is also important to see the urgency of the need to protect your planet from annihilation.

4 & 5. We reveal at this time, that our representatives, invisible though they may be, stand within your secret councils, and register the hidden plans of every government. We evaluate the long-range effect of those plans upon other nations and the effects for good or ill upon the greatest number of persons. We shall do all in our power through natural means to prevent nuclear war upon the planet. We are capable of reversing a missile and returning it to its launching base. This we may be forced to do if present plans prevail, for humanity will have all that it can bear in coping with nature unleashed. The arighting of a planetary body and all of the related effects are more than enough.

These are times to ask yourselves, "Where are we going,

and what are we headed for?" Events of such portent are so near, literally, at your doorstep, there remains no time for involvement in the destruction of one another. Be aware of the aura of urgency that surrounds your world.

**I Am, the Apostle**
**Philip**

## Points to Ponder
### -or-
### (Group Discussion)

I. The Saturnian Council.
2. The urgency of the Councils of Heaven.
3. The two potentials for worldwide disaster.
4. The invisible Statesmen.
5. The advanced technology of other worlds.

## NOTES:

# 7:00 AM The Sixth Day Millions of Space Craft

## by Klala

Greetings in the Light of the Beloved One. This is the voice of Ashtar. We have the contact, our beam is upon you. We are stationed over you and we have you on our screen. We are now releasing you to the great Space Commander and Master of Dynamics of energy and force. We have anticipated the moment of his coming, and his words. We now turn this communication over to Klala.

1. My name is Klala. I greet you in the Light of the Radiant One. I come as a messenger from the Alliance of Galaxies of outer Space. I represent the combination of all the energies beaming upon the planet earth, at its time of ascension into a New World Order. Millions upon millions of space craft now encircle your planet within your own magnetic force-field. Many represent your own Solar System, many others come from far off universes serving under their own Tribunal, but all are coordinated through Commander Matton and the Ashtar Command. Commander Ashtar has graciously introduced me this morning and prepared you for my words.

2. Great devastation will come to the planet earth if your present scientific endeavors proceed without control. Modern

channeling of the great planetary energies into self-destruction cannot be permitted under Universal Law. That Law is higher than any of the Tribunals that represent any galaxy.

3. Great force-fields of power and energy are inherent within the earth to provide the necessary support of life and nature. The Creator has designed our worlds and invested them with all the necessities for the ongoing and evolution of life. Science should be the proper study of isolating those energies and applying them for the benefit of humanity. Unfortunately, upon the earth, in your scheme of things, the energy within the atom of order has been disbursed into disorder, disturbing the atomic life of the planet into chaos. An expansion of this program beyond your ionosphere to areas of Space is intolerable to other Worlds, and is restricted under the edict of the Great Central Government.

4. I repeat, millions of craft are in orbit around your planet. Some monitor the thoughts and evolution of individuals as they progress to higher levels of evolvement. Other craft continually measure scientific expression and monitor the application of new revelation. Communications, wavelengths, that encircle your globe, pass through our own systems remotely controlled by what you call Mother Ships. Other forms of craft fulfill constant missions of manning the faultlines and volcanic areas. Any changes noted bring an instant alert.

There are thousands of lesser craft that are designed to be at the instant availability for any purpose by those of us who walk your planet as representatives of our love and good will toward men of earth. Coordinated patrols have been heavily concentrated in the past decade, in cleansing the atmospheres of the nefarious influences and those who oppose the program of Light. This action is now in a closing phase, clearing the advent of interplanetary relations and exchange.

5. Through the years, measured portions of scientific knowledge have been released to the planet earth that have ultimately led into your present activities in Space. That which

has gone before represents a minimum of that which may and will be released in the future. There is much misunderstanding in many fields regarding the dynamics of energy and magnetic force-fields, and lines of force within the earth.

6. Advancement is presently halted pending the settlement of the problems of interplanetary peace. We do have the authority under Universal Principles, as well as the technical ability of total nullification of nuclear weapons. We do not and may not intrude into international, national or personal karma, but beyond that point where the Great Law is satisfied, we can and will intervene in nuclear hostilities.

7. Tremendous themes of spiritual advancement are now due to come to mankind. With this enlightenment will come much scientific inspiration and breakthrough. When transmutation is complete, a remnant of your people will find themselves relocated in the great City-Craft that orbit the upper heavens, as the Guardians nullify the destructive radioactivity of your atmosphere, and heal the planetary wounds in preparation of a New Day. This is the Divine Order of things. Metamorphosis is inevitable and inescapable, for that which is corruptible may not inherit that which is incorruptible. The chaos of disorder of the atomic structure of all creation shall be magnetized into order once again, and new life will begin on a level in harmony with Universal Brotherhood.

In the Light of the Radiant One, I conclude my words. Friends of earth, Adonai.

—Klala

## Points to Ponder
### –or–
### (Group Discussion)

I. The vast scope of the Guardian Action.
2. Universal Law is higher than any Galactic Tribunal.
3. The proper study of science.
4. The various missions of Space Craft.
5. Planetary ignorance of the dynamics of energy.
6. Karma *vs* intervention.
7. The Divine Order of things.

## NOTES:

# 11:00 AM The Sixth Day We Must Be Invited

## by Kadar Monka

**1 & 2.** Monka speaking to Tuella. Greetings, child of Light! I am Monka, the Protector of the Earth, and representative of Earth at the Great Tribunals. I am interested in the link-up between souls of Earth and your Space Friends who serve as intermediaries between Earth and the Higher Councils. I can say that it is imperative that these link-ups are made with your Space Friends before the disasters come. Contacts attempted at the very hour of rescue may be "too little and too late." Now is the time to build up compatible force-fields for future coexistence and alignment for joint activity. Your vibrations must be lifted to a level that will intermingle with our higher energies without stress on either frequency. The greatest harmony is maintained by a thorough mastery of emotional balance on your part. A greater stability of thought levels, through habitual attitudes of mental control. and emotional control, builds toward a high frequency to establish rapport and a greater affinity between us. You have been warned by others that frequency factors can bring shock to the physical when boarding our craft. Human auric energy fields must be in harmony with Divine Love and the Universal Brotherhood, which is the frequency of the Space Brothers. This lack of emotional constancy represents the greatest problem in preparation for boarding our craft, and enjoying fellowship with us.

**3. & 4.** Advance preparations are necessary to prepare the lower bodies for alignment with the new energy densities now entering your atmospheres, and life in the New Age, as well as exposure to us in our craft. Therefore, one must begin NOW to have absolute personal control over all negative emotions and "feelings," lest the personal frequency drop below that level required for contact with us. We cannot compel you or force you to desire this contact with the Higher Forces, but once that desire has germinated within your own Being, we may then respond to it with our enabling beams and force-field around the human form, which blend the desire of your soul with the desire we have for a contact of spirit. Therefore, the more accustomedness that is developed to our presence and our penetration of your thinking, the easier it will be for more and more to accept us and invite our assistance.

**5.** It is important for Earth Beings to realize that we must be invited in to your vibrational pattern. Under Universal Law we do not have the right to intrude our presence into your lives and frequencies without your permission. This fact should be made known so that all will understand that the representatives of the Solar Cross Federation stand in the shadows ready to assist, and to uphold, to teach, and to encourage mankind upon the Earth. But we must be invited, we must be called into your thinking, your quiet times and upreach, that we might blend our frequencies toward compatibility, and cooperation in the mission that is ahead for all of us.

I am a veteran of this program, having devoted all of my energies to its ongoing success. My heart and soul are dedicated to the upliftment of humanity and the betterment of life upon Earth, and to the uniting of all planets in a Confederation of Peace and Goodwill. These are not only my goals, but the goals of every other member of the tribunals of Space, who stand ready to uphold righteousness upon the planet.

**6 & 7.** There has been a great cleansing in the heavens.

Those forces that have sought to destruct and literally destroy, if that were possible, the plans of the Higher Ones for the salvation of Earth and its inhabitants, those forces have been curtailed. We can report to you that a great sweeping action by the entire Space Confederation has just been completed.

The heavens now stand ready to exert a unified action upon the challenges that Earth must face in the coming decade. A program is now being launched, embodying the concerted action for the cleansing of Earth's vibrations and force-fields, through the radiations of the incoming Seventh Ray.

You may therefore expect to experience a tightening around your own electromagnetic fields, that will produce within your being a sensitivity to those emotions which lessen your spiritual alignment. By this, I mean that you are going to become more sensitive to your personal reactions to situations on the emotional level. Your consciousness will become more aware of weaknesses of the "feeling" nature, and you will begin to "police" these weaknesses and overcome them. Enter into this cleansing of one's Being in a cooperative way, for all the kingdoms of Creation, as well as the planet itself, will experience this cleansing simultaneously. Listen to the still, small voice of heart and soul and conscience, and flow with them and the incoming energies, toward a positive, spiritual life! These influences have already begun. Those of you who are committed to service in the Light will find yourselves walking with a giant's tread. Those who are antagonistic to the frequencies of Light will be overcome by those frequencies and translated to a dimension beyond them.

8 & 9. You will strive for perfection, although you may never have done so before. This desire for perfection is a natural spiritual trait, for those created in the image of the Radiant One. This striving for outward perfection of the Perfect Being Within shall be greatly assisted from this moment onward. This holy striving fosters a dissatisfaction with anything less than the quality of the Christ Presence within. This

Divine Unction is beginning to move within souls where it has never shown evidence of its influence before. You will see this in your neighbors, in your coworkers, in your fellow human beings whom you meet with from day to day. You will discern the results of the powerful cleansing ray as it penetrates the planetary rays. You will sense it within your own family and within your own crowd. There will be a sensitivity toward the good, and, unfortunately, an intensifying of the darkness surrounding those who resist this change. Those who refuse by human will, to accept change cannot receive our help. We can do nothing for them. They shall be taken to a place of waiting, where they and others like them shall wait together until such time as they can become willing within their being, to change. But this shall be in another place, in another time, and not part of the future program for earth.

We of the Space Commands have waited and worked, for countless ages to see this day when these cleansings could begin to take place. I, Monka, a representative for the Earth in the Higher Tribunals, find great happiness to be able to report to you that as this cleansing carries forward, those who cooperatively yield themselves to it, will find great blessings expanding throughout their entire life. The blessings of God must be sought. His Presence must be invited. So "Seek the Lord, while He may be found," and "Call upon Him while He is near." Do not wait until chaos is upon you. Now is the time. This is the day to begin your preparations against those days.

10. I am Monka. I speak for all those in cooperative action of the Intergalactic Space Program. We send our beams of brotherly Love upon all of you who are cooperating with the Light, for this becomes the equilibrium that holds all things in place. The Love of the Father and Love for one another can hold the earth in its position for eternity. If enough souls of Earth can radiate this vibration of Love, in great power, this transition in time, inaugurating a New Age and a New Cycle can proceed smoothly with a minimum of alignment adjust-

ments for mankind. Think on these things as you face the coming decade. In the Light of the Radiant One,

**I Am,**
**—Kadar Monka**

## Points to Ponder
### –or–
### (Group Discussion)

1. Begin NOW.
2. Compatible frequency imperative.
3. Emotional stability and harmony prerequisite for rescue.
4. Enabling beams to enhance desire for harmony.
5. Contact must be invited and sought.
6. Cleansing of upper spheres completed.
7. Earth cleansed by the Violet Ray.
8. Transmutation.
9. The laggards have a place prepared.
10. Love is the "glue" of the Universe.

## NOTES:

# Section Four
# World Deliverance

## Angels of the Apocalypse

The sky is dark but not with fright,
It forms a canopy of truth and might.
By the millions they have come—
The glory of their mission, a sight so rare
With great whirlwinds and clouds
Of silvery ships materializing out of the air.
To rescue mankind is their intention,
A Love like this defies description!

Without your understanding how,
Skies open wide and in a flash—
You are transported high above
Traveling in the realms of Light.
Passing constellations great,
As tiny earth recedes from sight.
You sense the presence of the Guardians
And the Father's Abounding Love.

Behold His Plan for your deliverance
Unfolding majestically from above.
But you must understand that help
Can only come if fear has changed to Love.
Other spheres suspended in the sky
Spinning rhythmically pass us by.
God's Other Worlds, His own to claim—
All are numbered, all are named.

On one of these you'll stay awhile,
Become renewed, transformed as Light,
Completely perfect in His sight!
When you return to beautiful earth,
Renewed with its own divine rebirth
Transformed like us, through Godly grace,
You'll know at last the meaning of

"Thy Kingdom come, Thy will be done,"
On earth—with Love
As it is in the heavens above.

—Eileen Schoen

# 3:00 PM The Sixth Day
# Hold the World
# to Your Heart

### by Paul the Venetian

Greetings to the children of Limitless Love. I am known as Paul the Venetian. I come from out of the pink ray of Love and Life. I come to you in the gentleness and the softness of the vibration of Love, from the Most High Plane. I am filling this room with my pink ray as it swirls round and about your physical form and the chair where you are seated. I weave round and about your being, pulsing vibrations of the Love of God.

I ask you for this moment to visualize your world globe. Visualize upon it, the continents, the great bodies of water, and the land masses upon it. Now take the swirling pattern of Divine Love with which I have encircled you, and *hold the world to your heart* with both of your hands and arms round about it. Let Love which I pour through your heart chakra, penetrate all of the land masses, the continents, the mountains, the deserts, the high places and the low places, the great oceans and the bodies of water, the great cities and the plains, the populated places and the deserted places, the cold frozen north and the warm tropical south, and let the Love of God flow from

111

your heart to the world and all thereon.

Let this Divine Love which at this moment is being poured through your four lower bodies, your entire being, let this Love go forth to every man, woman and child wherever they may be. I send this pink ray of Divine Love to every living soul of America. Let us expand our Love Ray, and project this Love northward, throughout Canada and from the length and the breadth of this hemisphere and fill it with Love and flow Divine Love out to all of Life. Let us flow this Divine Love upon the ships at sea, on the oceans and the great bays, and the great seas to everyone who is at sea. Let the Love of God flow round and about every ship and vessel everywhere the keeping, protecting, beautifying pink ray of the Love of God.

Then up into Europe and the northernmost parts, into the nation of Russia, and up into Siberia, and all over the continent, to the north and to the south of it, to the east and to the west of it, I shed forth through thy being this projection of the pink ray of the Love of God, everywhere upon the planet. Down throughout Australia, all through the African continent, and all around through the Orient and the great land of India, I enclose them all in my arms of Love, and I project the pink ray of the Love of God through thy being at this hour, and send it round and round and about the entire planet to hold it together, to keep it together, to exalt Love in the human heart.

I send Love, the Love of the pink ray, to all the world leaders of all nations. I shed forth through all of the national governments the pink ray of the Love of God and brotherhood and Love for one another, that mankind may awaken and come to know his brother in the Love of God. I call forth the Angels of the Celestial Kingdom, great legions upon legions of angels, to encircle the globe and to weave round and about it a great geometric pattern, an interlocking pattern of Love, that mankind will Love one another. As the Love of God prevails throughout the Universes in beauty and harmony, so shall the pink ray of Divine Love be flooded upon the earth, from the hands of the

Angels who answer my cell and do my bidding. I administer the energies of Love to the planet. It is my heart which bleeds forth everywhere at this hour, a new baptism of Love through my order that has gone forth, to increase and to step up the vibrations of the Love Ray throughout this solar system.

I call for Love Meditations, where souls shall gather together to measure the depth and the status of their Love, and the quality of their Love, one for another. I call for the great ray of Love to cleanse and to penetrate every beating heart, with humility, and openness, and brokenness in the presence of the Love of God.

The Love Ray can solve every problem that besets your world. Love is the answer. Anything less than Perfect Love is the problem, but Love is the answer.. Beloved soul, are you motivated by Love in your personal affairs? Are you motivated by Love in your community affairs? Are you motivated by Love in your national affairs? Are you motivated by Love in international relationships and decisions? Anything less than Perfect Love is not only a part of the problem but a producer of the problem, but Love is the answer. The Love of God within your heart, operating, motivating every thought and word and deed, can END ALL WAR FOREVER! Love operating on the human level can bring Peace and Harmony to all the other kingdoms and bring balance to your planet. But anything less than Perfect Love can bring destruction through disharmony.

Love in action in the affairs of humanity can bring a smooth and a beautiful transition to your planet as you enter the new dimension and the new expression of Love in the Golden Age. But anything less than Perfect Love can forfeit your participation in these beautiful things. My call has gone forth to every beating heart, a call for Love to be given its natural place in your lives, and your affairs, in your future. Lay aside the clutter of lesser demands, the harshness, the coldness, and the callousness of indifference. Open thy being and call upon the Heavenly Father to LOVE THROUGH YOU, AND

THIS HE WILL DO. This is my call—to Love!

This is my benediction, the gridwork and the pattern of the Ray of Love that the Angels have placed around your world. I hold it in position. It is lowered enough for you to reach, and pull down into your life and your world. It is NOT too late! There is still time to shed Love abroad into all planetary affairs, and all details of your personal lives. You are in embodiment that you might learn the lessons of Love.

I have spoken to you from out of the flowing spiral of the pink ray of Divine Love.

**I Am**
**Paul the Venetian**

*This message of Love was received in one of the most beautiful vibrations ever experienced. The words fell like pink rose petals, in the gentleness of the theme. The delivery was a soft, gentle whisper, and the pace was very slow. The message should be read very very slowly, and softly, with long pauses represented by the punctuation.*

• • •

*The beautiful meditation as given, encircling the globe with your arms as you enter the visualization of projecting Love (which is Light) into every area of our world, is recommended as a spiritual exercise for both individuals and groups.*

• • •

*In the weeks just previous to the full moon vigil of August and the weeks immediately following, there was a severe Red Alert status throughout the Space Confederation. I later learned that many other spiritual messengers, friends of mine, had also been alerted. The status was lifted in mid-September. It is the feeling of this messenger that this great outpouring of Love from this wonderful Being, administered by the Angels at that point in time, alleviated some crisis then present.*

—Tuella

# The Descent of the Guardians

## by Space Commander Athena

Good evening, Tuella. I am coming in the ray of the Divine Mother and in Her Name. I am Space Master and Commander Athena. I serve at the great control board of the mother ship of the Ashtar Command. With our beam I cover you with Love and Light.

**1.** It is with a heavy heart that I must yield my thoughts to concern for the planet as the coming changes begin to manifest. It is one thing to consider and to dwell on the glory that comes after, and it truly is and will be a great glory to come, but it is another matter to look upon those whom I love so dearly, whose lives upon the planet have been in my care and under my guidance for many embodiments, now standing on the brink of planetary karma. Gladly would I exchange places with all of you, if that were possible.

**2.** But as you have followed your own indwelling Light down through the years through many trials and testings, you have learned, and learned the lesson well, to be overcomers by the Grace of God that is given unto you. You have learned obedience through the things you have suffered. You have learned that the darkest night is always followed by the dawn. You have learned that in the time of deepest test the nearness of His Presence was your reward. Think of these coming times as change comes to you, as another opportunity to become an overcomer and a pillar in the house of your God. Another opportunity to know Him in the fellowship of His suffering and the blessedness of His Presence as a present help in time of trouble. None of His little ones will go through these changes alone. His Angels and His Representatives will be beside you to whisper in your ear, with guidance and deliverance whenever and wherever it is needed.

There was a time when His children came across the bottom of the sea, walking upon dry ground, while the waters parted to bid them pass by. The glory of His Presence with His little ones in the coming days will pale the former account in comparison, so great shall be His Hand of deliverance in the day of transition of your world. You shall be raised as Elijah was raised, lifted up as Jesus was lifted up, by the presence of the Guardians who wait. Those who have made their calling and election sure, can know that destruction will not come nigh thee, but that His Hand shall be extended to thee through the presence of those who represent Him at the hour of your deliverance.

The attitudes of life are the deciding factors when that moment comes. It will be too late in that hour to suddenly reverse yourself and pretend new attitudes. These will have been built into the geometric patterns and the good works that surround every being. An attitude of love will be so interlaced into the electronic force-field of your being that none could miss its presence. Attitudes of selfishness and greed, or cruelty, are plainly to be seen within the force-field of humanity. Rebelliousness, disrespect, and corruption stand revealed, built into the very framework of the four lower bodies, through the long years of lesser motivations.

As we approach your world and your atmospheres, we are not left with these decisions, and for this we are thankful. Our operations have an impersonal overtone. The choice has already been made by each and every one by the incorporate attitudes of life. You have chosen whether to go or to stay, many times down through your lifetime; as you have chosen between the right and the wrong, enlightenment and density, spirituality and materialism, kindness and cruelty, selfishness and unselfishness. At that very moment that you have faced a choice of decision or in any of life's situations, you have been building toward your final choice soon to manifest.

5. For this cause therefore, is my heart saddened as I look upon these changes that must come. It has been said that only one tenth shall remain when these things are passed. This need not be so. No prophecy is fixed, but all prophecy is subject to the will of man, his decisions and his choices. It is not too late, even now, for a cleansing of the attitudes of life. By an act of will, to change the personal positions which do not lead to the way of life. Those who read my words in this little volume, may even now determine to align themselves with the principles and the purpose of Divine Light as it is shed upon the planet. A great Master once presented it in this way, "Choose ye this day whom ye will serve."

6. This is the point of the beginning of the end of things. Each individual unit of consciousness acting upon human freedom of choice, self determining to cast their energies into the battle for Light upon the earth. You simply begin where you are, and from this point on, at every moment of choice, at every crossroad of decision, cast your lot on the side of that which is right, that which is wholesome, that which is pure and that which is clean. And you go on from there as you ask for guidance from on high to show you the way and lead you onward into more Light. As you begin this new adventure and reverse your attitudes of life, you are building into the grid-work and the framework of your own force-field that which shall shine through and be seen by the reaping angels when they appear.

That which is done in secret shall be rewarded openly by the Heavenly Father. Now is the time. We cannot know how much time remains. The universe and all therein stand alerted and ready. My question to you this day is this: "Are YOU ready for the coming of the Guardians?" "Will YOU qualify for the coming rescue?" "Will YOU be found in the remnants that remain?" YOU are the Master of your fate, and YOU are the only one who can answer my questions. YOU are the only one who can determine the action that will be taken WHEN WE COME. Will YOU be ready for that day? I pray that the Light within you and around you will help you in your choice. I Am Lady Master Athena of the Ashtar Command.

—Athena

## Points to Ponder
### –or–
### (Group Discussion)

I. The brink of planetary karma..
2. The lesson of life–overcoming (Mastery).
3. The great liftoff.
4. Attitudes of life are the building blocks of future events.
5. All prophecy is subject to change.
6. Finding the way out of confusion.
7. Three vital questions.

## NOTES:

# 7:00 AM The Seventh Day Keep Your Eyes on the Skies

## by Lord Arcturus

My name is Arcturus from the planet of the same name. I am coming to you this morning on a powerful beam from outer space. My words are projected to you through the Ashtar Command Monitor. Kuthumi has kindly granted my request to speak as a representative of outer space. This is a great honor to me that my words will be included in the volume that he sends forth. I speak on behalf of all my friends and yours, in the Alliance and the Brotherhood of Interplanetary Fellowship.

1. The situation that has been accelerating upon Earth has been a cause of great concern to all of us who follow the events very closely. We have monitored the planetary disturbances and the potential for greater ones. We have given the utmost time and attention to your international affairs, because of the diversion of nuclear atomic energy into weapons of destruction. The planet of Arcturus and our entire constellation has been in constant support of the volunteer program ministering to Earth. The patrols and fleets from Arcturus are an ever-present unit of the Guardian Action that protects your planet.

2. We come with our thousands of ships and thousands upon thousands of willing volunteers, who have come the great

121

distance between us to be with you and to help you in the travail of your new birth into the Aquarian age of expression. The processes involved for your planet in this great event, will require assistance from your brothers of other galaxies and other systems. My beloved friends of Earth, you cannot stand alone in that which is to come. You cannot reject our loving offer of hope and specific guidance. In preparedness for the despair that could ensue, our Alliance has unified its forces and in a unanimous decision of the highest council in Space, it was agreed that our fleets be alerted and ready from that moment on for momentary response to the need of humanity.

This means that every county, every province and state, of every nation; every province of every republic, is now systematically patrolled by representatives of our Alliance. It means that great beams and cosmic rays, called forth by the Lords of your solar system, are being centralized and beamed directly upon the Earth by these regional representatives, of the Guardians from outer space. It means that all opposition to the will of the Divine Father and the Hierarchy of your system and its Great Central Government has been removed and rendered inoperative for this important cycle of time.

4 & 5. Our technology is readied to superimpose our frequencies over your television and radio broadcasting systems if necessary, to reach the masses in the quickest possible manner. We can also extend our frequencies into your telephone lines for a brief message, but your telephones would then be unusable thereafter. We have systems similar to your public address systems, available from the smaller scout ships, which operate with a volume and power unheard of in your technology. We have many ways of reaching quantities of persons simultaneously. We project into your thinking at this very date, that fear of us and our presence or our appearance, or lack of understanding of our motivation, will combine to produce such a negative field around your physical form that we would be unable to assist you. You must enlarge your thinking and

expand your knowledge of our purpose and our intermediary action under God and the Hierarchy under Heaven. We come in their name to serve you, our brothers of Earth. We cannot promise you another decade. We cannot even promise you all of this one. Your destiny is in your hands.

6. I am burdened for the children who must be exposed to the dangers in your world. I am heartbroken when I reflect on the past quarter of a century and the great toll of young lives that have been taken in war. Thousands upon thousands of young lives were thrown back into eternity without ever having a chance for expression and growth. I appeal to mankind to consider the children as you deliberate and choose the path that you would take. Consider if this is the path you would want your children to follow. Is this the destiny for the children you love and the children you know? All too many walk the planet with scars of war that can never heal in this lifetime. Scars upon the psyche which can never find relief throughout this embodiment. Much has been written of the suffering of the Earth itself, and the nations, and the adults of the people. But can you find it in your hearts to think for a moment of the children of your world and the effects of atomic warfare upon the inner levels of their soul memory? Not only in this world, but the next?

7. I reveal to you in this release that we shall call for the children first. For the children are guiltless and the children are the victims of the madness of the adult world surrounding them. We shall make a place on our ships and our places of refuge for the children, first. These souls who have dared to enter your world at such a time as this, deserve our love and care first of all. For they do not know hatred until they are taught to hate. They do not know to kill until they are taught to kill. They do not know of mass destruction until they are taught to destroy. Each living soul has its identifying ray, its link with its own personal record on our great computers. Your children are not lost when they are with us. They will be res-

cued first, and await your coming. Many thousands of your children are special souls, who have come to progress, to unfold, and participate in the dawn of a New World.

The Space Commanders and those who serve with them in the heavens surrounding your planet, have been engaged in an intensive program of sweeping, cleansing action, by the direct Order of the Great Central Government. We will fill your skies the moment that our presence and your physical rescue is necessary. Truly it can be said, "Look up, for your redemption draweth nigh." I would say, "Keep your eyes on the skies," when catastrophe overtakes you, for we are there. We ARE there."'

I have come to you in an offer of Universal Peace and Goodwill. I call upon mankind of Earth to lay down your weapons of holocaust. I am the voice and Lord of Arcturus and Commander in Chief of its great Space Armada.

I Am
—Arcturus

## Points to Ponder
### –or–
### (Group Discussion)

I. The planet Arcturus and the Guardian Action.
2. Assistance from Space is vital.
3. The worldwide canopy of patrol.
4. Everyone can be reached in a time of crisis.
5. Fear is detrimental to rescue.
6. Consider the children's fate!
7. In a mass evacuation, the children go first.

## NOTES:

# 11:00 AM The Seventh Day When Your Need Is Greatest, They Will Be There

## by Brother James, The Apostle

1. This is a great pleasure to speak with one who has served the Light so faithfully for many lifetimes. I am the brother of Jesus the Christ. I am known as James. I have many other names, but I come in my identity as the Apostle James, and Jesus of Nazareth was my brother. We were raised in the same household and I followed Him in His ministry. I have known you in that lifetime and many lifetimes since then. I recognize you, Tuella, and I honor the Christ Presence within you. I now serve the Light upon the planet in my world as teacher. I speak and work through many dedicated ones at this time. I have overshadowed one in whom I have invested the momentum of a portion of my being, whom you will one day meet. Kuthumi has kindly invited me to contribute a few words to the World Messages. I am delighted to do this, for I see them as a vital link to the years of the coming decade.

2. As I prepare to share my thoughts, may I call your

126

attention to the recent volcanic eruption in northwest America. This brought great concern, and the world media featured the coverage for considerable time. Precious lives are missing and have not yet been found. This occurrence could be likened to a brief preview of headlines that are to come. This was an isolated incident, but in the future, events of this magnitude will occur in concurrent sequence in diverse places. Your media will be at a loss to report them all. Television reports will fill the day in continuing attempts to cover these events, so recurrent will be the disasters, so widespread the locations.

3 & 4. These have been referred to as changes that must come. The restlessness of the inner earth which awakens the sleeping volcanoes to belch forth their living fire, is the same momentum which manifests elsewhere as tremors or earthquakes of small or large magnitude. Tidal waves and intense weather abnormalities, shifting plates of land beneath the oceans, and the quivering of the mountains, could take place in concerted action, so that humanity would have nowhere to run, nowhere to turn and no sense of direction or idea of what they must do to save themselves. Panic could grip the hearts of people, resulting in calls upon God for deliverance. *IT IS IN HOURS SUCH AS THESE THAT YOUR SKIES WILL FILL WITH THE SHIPS OF YOUR BROTHERS FROM OTHER REALMS.*

5. As all are aware, there is also the ever-present danger that a small group of men shall detonate the initial action of nuclear disaster. Unless there were no divine intervention from the Guardians, the very planet itself would suffer total annihilation. But ere that initial release goes forth, a warning will be broadcast upon the Higher Ethers for those who have accustomed their sensitivity to the higher frequencies of communication. Whether in a voice, or in a dream, or a vision or whatever manner, the elect shall receive that warning to prepare themselves for momentary evacuation. When the elect (volunteers to planet earth) have been gathered from the four winds and

127

returned to their fold, the remaining stages of the program of the Guardians will take place.

6. None can tell when that moment will be, any more than any of you could with any certainty determine its time, for no man knoweth when that dire set of circumstances shall manifest. Therefore, the Guardians are on the alert, ever on the alert, listening, watching, recording, standing by, waiting and ever prepared for immediate action. Gird up thyselves, we would say in my day as a fisherman in Galilee. We would gird up our loins for action. My message to the world is a call to gird up your souls for spiritual action in the days of calamity. Be ye as men who wait for their Lord, knowing not at what hour of what day these things shall come to pass. These are perilous times. The threats and dangers are not illusions; they are real. They could be imminent. The detonating of any first nuclear missile, even for testing purposes, in many areas, could precipitate a sequence of geological reactions upon the earth and the ionosphere surrounding it, setting loose unspeakable and indescribable catastrophes.

The heavenly Tribunals and the Alliance of powers in Space are coordinating their constant efforts, even at this very moment, to forestall such eventualities and all acts or intentions of nuclear hostilities.

7. Between the time of decision and action, the moments will be very brief. It is that brief moment of time, when the skies will fill with the craft of your Brothers of other worlds to rescue humanity. Their time for entering and accomplishing their mission will be crucially short. There must be an inner understanding within the hearts of mankind that the Guardians have come to assist them in their time of trouble. They have patrolled your heavens for thousands of years with every effort geared toward this eventuality, when the planet Earth would enter its transition into a new orbit of total change. The transition period can bring chaos to your world; nevertheless, it need not be individual chaos. Many voices have flooded the

planet with the messages of your Protectors. Many channels have been used by the Great Ones and your Space Friends to give an assurance of their presence and their help.

8. It is proposed that the rescue of souls from off the planet in a time of peril, from whatever cause, will take place in three phases. The first phase shall be the secret removal of those elect whose dedication to Light on Earth has made our Program possible. These shall be called to that secret place where they shall be taken on high to a place prepared. Then shall come the call to all of those of Light, all of those with awareness and ears to hear, and faith to believe and courage to understand that which is taking place. The scope of this phase of the evacuation will be tremendous and include a far greater number than might be imagined. They will respond and follow directives and guidance under leadership of certain ones. These that have prepared themselves shall be lifted by the smaller ships to those platforms of immensity now in orbit in your skies.

The final phase, when the two groups are safe, and as remaining time permits, shall be the call to mass evacuation. Following the accomplishment of the first two missions, many who remain will have become willing believers in all of these things. In this final mass action, the children shall be lifted first and then, with the multitude, taken to a place prepared.

When the planet is made new again, cleansed and beautiful once more, those who are worthy shall be returned to a new life in a new age, on a planet made new, in the fellowship and the companionship of those who delivered them.

Perhaps as you read of these things the thoughts are overwhelming to you, as you rest in the quiet of your home environment, but the situation can change in the twinkling of an eye. Although my words may have little significance to you at this time, in the day when these things begin to happen, a memory of my words will be brought forth from inner consciousness.

9. Cultivate inner peace. Learn the art of listening with the

inner ear. When you have spoken with your Lord, and come to an end of your prayer, linger awhile. Cultivate the art of listening with the inner ear. Become attentive with the inner being to the pulse and the heartbeat of the Universe. The God to whom you pray is within you, as close as your breath. I Am That I Am will whisper within as you practice the Presence of the guidance of the inner Divinity. This is where you must turn when it would seem the world is crumbling around you. Within your being, call upon that I Am Presence, the Divine Indwelling, to send help and deliverance for you and your loved ones.

10. My beloved brothers and sisters, beyond that midnight hour a great dawn awaits the planet. The glory of a new day of Light and Brotherhood of all worlds. Begin now to develop your awareness of these Other Sheep of the Father, these Other Children of the Father filled with Divine attributes and spiritual purposes, even as you and yours. Let your love flow upward and outward to these dedicated Guardians, patrolling your skies, like watchmen on the walls, for your sake and your safety. Send your love to them, and your gratitude, for the Father hath sent them. In that hour when your need is greatest, they shall be there!

An Apostle of Jesus the Christ, I Am,

—Brother James

## Points to Ponder
### –or–
## (Group Discussion)

I. An "overshadowing" Master.
2. Recurrent and widespread disasters.
3. The restlessness of the inner earth.
4. Our ever-present help from above.
5. The warning of the elect.
6. Dangers could be imminent.
7. The moment of action for the Guardians.
8. The three phases of evacuation.
9. Become attentive with the inner being.
10. Other sheep of the Father, not of this fold.

## NOTES:

## The Ultimate Weapon

They spoke of ways and means
To stop proliferation of the bomb.
So ponderous with knowledge scientific
Did they endlessly exclaim—
Who will make it next?
O don't you know it is of God
Designed to service all of life,
Not to destroy the perfect patterns
of His Work?

Cannot one voice be raised
To the heights of protest great
That will pierce the ears,
Lay bear the hearts
Of those so wantonly engaged
In victory through slaughter
Of each other, man on earth,
Their brother!

Rather would they find a use for
That ultimate of weapons great,
Designed to penetrate each heart
And burn through channels of the brain;
Created to keep God's plan in motion,
Till all are one again, no separation.
This luminous flame of GOD'S GREAT LOVE—
That ultimate weapon...from above!

—Eileen Schoen

# 3:00 PM The Seventh Day
# The Impersonal Frequencies

### by Space Master Hatonn

Thank you, Tuella, for opening your door to receive my words. I have come at the invitation of Lord Kuthumi, my good friend and brother. I am with him this day to honor your vigil and assist in this special time of outpouring and blessing. I am Hatonn of the Space Council. I send my greetings to all in the Light of the Radiant One. It is my pleasure to come and I have anticipated this contact for the ongoing Light.

1. We of the Space Commands do have tremendous plans organized, completely ready for action, for a mass evacuation. As we have considered all the facts, and weighed in the balance all of the possibilities and the probabilities, it is the conclusion of the great Tribunal that the evacuation will be necessary. We are permitting you this release for the Tribunal in my name, to advise the people of Earth that mass evacuation will take place for all of those whose spiritual advancement makes compatibility with us possible.

2 & 3. Our ships are environments of harmony and peace. There is quietness, cooperation and dignity. There is courtesy and devotional awareness within each being. This is the only attitude capable of continuance in the vibrational atmosphere

present within our space ships. The frequencies are so very high that they would destroy any vibrations of a lesser nature. It is not a matter of saying "This one may come, or this one must stay," it is of frequencies and vibrations. Just as a block of ice is melted and loses its form, its density, its appearance, within the vibration of higher temperatures, so it is that in the presence of the higher frequencies, they can do naught but decimate the density, the form, and the appearance of the lower frequencies. This is why, throughout the planet, as souls go about the pursuit of Light and Divine Oneness, there is a marking star, shining forth from the forehead of the being. This becomes an identification to us at the time of evacuation. You will read of this star, in the vision of John recorded in your Bible. This inevitable separation has nothing to do with our personal desires in the matter. It is a question of frequencies and vibration. Those who have learned to live in love, and to apply an attitude of love to all situations, have thus prepared themselves for these days of turmoil, though perhaps they knew it not. For love of fellow man as a manifestation of the Presence of the Love of God, in the vibration of one in embodiment, is the highest frequency on the four lower planes. It is that point of union and compatibility with the planes that are above. It is at that meeting point of Love, that we can mingle with you and accept you into our midst and our ships for rescue.

4. Perfect love casteth out fear. Perfect love is love to man of all levels, of all galaxies of all the universes. Perfect love brings acceptance of us into your hearts. The presence of fear within your being will hinder your own evacuation in the time of great trouble. Therefore, the call comes now, to all who read, and all who think on these things, to realize that the preparation for that hour is the preparation of thyself. A preparation of thy heart and the cleansing of thy attitude, that perfect love to all beings, both of your world and mine, shall be found within you. There must be an acceptance of the presence of the Christ within all men, of any race, of any creed, or any

church, though yours differ, or of any color, realizing that the coats of skin are but an exterior manifestation. Unless this perfect love abides in you, you cannot abide within the higher frequencies of the upper planes.

Thus, with great love flowing from our hearts to you at this time, we would plead with you in the name of the Radiant One, that you would rethink your positions, that you would set a watch upon your spoken words regarding your brother or your sister, that you would most of all, control and discriminate carefully the thoughts that you entertain regarding your fellow man. For in that measure that you mete out judgment to them, that measure will return unto you, in that hour when you will stand in need of mercy and intervention.

5. I, Hatonn, Teacher and Master of the Higher Worlds, and speaker for the great Solar Tribunals of the Space Federation, I speak to you individually as one human soul who reads my words, and I call you to raise your level of living. Expand your horizon of love. Not only to include those that are near and dear to you, but your neighbor on the street, your coworker in your career, the leaders of your area, the men and women of your central government. Shed your attitude of love upon all as you would your very own. As each individual one of you expands your love and lets it flow into wider circles, the vibration of Light around each one, will ascend into higher octaves of Light. As many are thus occupied, in these years immediately ahead, especially these early years of the decade, such a glow of Love and Light will arise from the lower planes so intensely, that we will be able to gear down our own presence, and come into a position of the blending of our frequencies and bring a mass evacuation to pass with a minimum of difficulty and disturbance to all.

The planet Earth must enter its period of cleansing. As this cleansing takes place, it will be a time of great upheaval in many places, that the human element could not sustain. There are certain areas that may be considered as safer than others in these times of change, but in the event of the launching of nuclear atomic explosions upon the planet, there could be no flesh saved, except through our presence and our evacuation of those who remain. The method to be used in the event of this great undertaking, will be to quietly and silently remove our workers and representatives first of all. These elect will have their private instructions. Mass evacuation will very possibly institute the use of a cosmic ray which acts producing levitation, teleporting the physical form into the craft. Only those of the higher frequencies of love and awareness can respond to these beams. History has recorded the use of these for you in the stories of Elijah and Beloved Jesus Sananda as they departed from the physical octave.

Please realize the impersonal nature of these procedures. It is a question of frequencies and vibrations AND THE ABSENCE OF ALL FEAR. We have a few other alternatives and methods, that may be utilized and the local situation and the need of the hour will determine the choice of method. But regardless of the method used, again I ask that you understand these are impersonal procedures which represent a meeting ground of frequencies as we enter your world and you enter ours.

This is the call of this book, that you prepare your souls. Grow into Light. Expand your love and beam a field of love around the planet. For this circle of love around your globe, can be termed as our "landing field" for your salvation.

I am Brother Hatonn, speaking to you in the name of the Radiant One. Adonai, Adonai, Adonai.

—Hatonn

## Points to Ponder
### –or–
## (Group Discussion)

I. Plans for a mass evacuation.
2. The high frequency of space craft environment.
3. Love is the highest frequency of the four lower planes.
4. Fear will hinder evacuation procedures.
5. The blending of frequencies.

## NOTES:

# 7:00 PM The Seventh Day
# Our Radiant One

## by Lord Kuthumi (The Apostle John)

Kuthumi speaks. I am coming to you tonight in my identity as John the Apostle. In those days when I walked the land with the Beloved Master, my heart thrilled to hear His Words, to be in His Presence, to sit beside Him. To ply my questions and receive His great wisdom and understanding. As one of the daughters of Philip, you were with us also. I have had many lifetimes, a few of great report, but nothing in my continuing experiences of evolution can ever compare to the days when I walked at the Master's side. My love for this great Being of Light cannot be measured in words, or described. It is the focal point of my existence, the atom around which my soul revolves.

As I close this symposium of guidance for the years before you, I desire to speak in my identity as John, the younger of the twelve. For my heart burns to speak of that Radiant Star, who descended from Celestial orbit to walk with men of earth. His Beloved Presence and His teachings have been received and respected with much honor and reverence throughout your solar system, may galaxies and other universes. It was Shan, the dark planet, where He was vilely put to death. Yet the teachings He brought and exemplified remain to this day.

The written account as it exists in present form has suffered much distortion, dilution, and revision, and the interpolation of unsympathetic minds. Nevertheless, there has remained a thread of the inner teachings that weave through human understanding down through the centuries. Hidden within the phrases and the passages, there is enough of the secret wisdom remaining, that any truly hungry heart that meditates upon His words, even in their present form, will find an awakening, a birth of awareness, an enlightenment, that will change the course of their lives. His words are still Light and the essence of Life.

4. As this cycle of time flows into another, and great cosmic rays penetrate your world, hidden wisdom is exposed for man's understanding. But in the pursuit of spiritual knowledge, and many pathways, be not so overcome that you would ignore the simple teachings of our Beloved Lord. Rather let them blend as one, and you will discover that this Great Avatar taught the inner wisdom in His simple way, that all of mankind could understand. None could deny His unction and His Mastery. The energies of His Being would flow throughout the countryside and down the sides of the hills, where hundreds and hundreds would gather to listen to Him speak the words of Life. Many of those listening, in the years that followed gladly laid down their lives or entered the lion's arena for their defense of His words, and you were one of those, my sister, who entered those arena gates.

5. The beauty of His countenance as He stood with arms outstretched to reason with His audience, to speak His parables and His simple descriptions of the kingdom of heaven, was an experience that is written indelibly upon my own soul for all eternity. I have since that time, come to a broader understanding of many of the mysteries that were hidden in His words. Those who presently study in depth the mysteries of life and birth, and the Great Law, and the cycles of evolution and all of these masterly subjects, that are now so boldly coming to light, so boldly being taught; if these students of today will return

once again to the words of the Beloved Lord, Jesus the Christ, they will find a warmth enveloping them, as with their own enlightened understanding they perceive the true meanings veiled in His words. Students of today will recognize the application of Universal Law in His miracles, the stream of cosmic verities within His parables, and evidence of Space craft throughout the record. His latter day discourses become easy reference in terms of the Guardian Beings who today surround your world. It is only to this generation, that faces the end of this cycle of time, that is given the great privilege of understanding His words. Too often in the mystery schools, circles and groups for occult discussion, there is a tendency to bypass the teachings of Jesus, the Great Lord.

6. It is true, because of the lateness of the record and the handling of unsympathetic translators, distortion is present. It is nevertheless not great enough to suppress the power of His utterances. When you explore a passage containing His words, close your eyes for meditation, and visualize yourself standing in the crowd that pressed around Him constantly. Feel the radiance and the magnitude of His mighty force-field of divine energy as He raises His hands to bless the crowd. In your time of meditation you may find that He is standing there beside your chair.

His Great Being knows no boundary. No planet can hold Him, no tomb could enclose Him, and He lives today, and visits those who love Him.

7. His Presence can stand beside a million different souls in one moment of time and yet suffer no loss of its own vibrant power. He can deliver His dictations through many blessed channels at one time in many different places, and yet each word bears the unmistakable stamp of His Presence. He is the Lord of the Planet and its Great Teacher. Down through the corridors of time, and many cultures and civilizations, we have known Him by many planetary names.

As the planet throws off its old mantle to enter the new

orbit of evolution, He will not leave those who love His Principles to endure alone. The Christ consciousness shall expand and manifest within every human life form and strive for expression and recognition, lest the very stones cry out.

**8.** My comments, as I close the cover of this little volume foursquare, are designed for one thrust, one idea, and that is that you will take the teachings of Jesus the Christ into the New Decade, and let Him walk before you. Let Him survey the terrain ere you pass by. For His feet know the Way. He has trod the Path. There is no experience that you must face, that He has not already entered and conquered. He will lead you and shelter you in His Love and bring you safely to your destiny. This is my plea, that as you turn your energies toward enlightenment, and search for understanding and guidance, that you might also read once again the words of the greatest story ever told.

I am Kuthumi, known in those days as

—John

## Points to Ponder
### –or–
## (Group Discussion)

I. John the Beloved Apostle.
2. Dark Shan, the only planet that rejected the Radiant One.
3. The distortions of the Gospels.
4. All truth is consistent with itself.
5. Secret wisdom is hidden in His words.
6. Practicing the Presence.
7. Can you name some other manifestations of the Great Soul?
8. Jesus Our Lord goes before us, so that anything that reaches us has been met by Him first, and touches us only by His permission. Rom. 8:28.

## NOTES:

# The Final Words

This is Ashtar greeting you with the sunrise, on this last morning of your vigil.

The deluge of Divine Love that has engulfed you these last twenty-four hours is shared with all of us, as we also are overcome with Love for the Heavenly Father and for all mankind.

You have realized that we have been impressing you for many hours with the words of the Beloved, 'I, if I be lifted up, will draw all men unto me.'

The Ashtar Command, and all of my fellow Commanders and the members of all of our fleets, serve in the Light of the Radiant One. Our dedication is to His Great Mission, which is much broader than His Mission to Earth. The scope of His Love and His teachings has penetrated many universes. The Love of the Radiant One is a nucleus and a center, a focus of creation, throughout infinity. This Love for Him who is the Light of the World, that fills your heart this beautiful sunrise is shared by all of the universes.

Yes, we have now closed the covers of the volume foursquare, as Kuthumi spoke so eloquently last night. The vision has descended into manifestations from the octaves of Light.

And now—the Heavenly Father holds it in His Hands.

Tuella, our command salutes you.

—Ashtar

# About The Author—Tuella

Tuella's "calling" as a Messenger of Light began in the early seventies with her channeling work commissioned personally by Ashtar on behalf of the Intergalactic Space Confederation. In addition to *Project World Evacuation,* her future works to be published by Inner Light include *Messengers For The Coming Decade, Ashtar—A Tribute, On Earth Assignment,* and *The Dynamics of Cosmic Telepathy.*